W9-BVB-675

JARED, THE SUBWAY GUY

JARED FOGLE

with Anthony Bruno

JARED, THE SUBWAY GUY

Winning Through Losing:

13 Lessons for Turning
Your Life Around

St. Martin's Pres New York

The names of some individuals have been changed.

JARED, THE SUBWAY GUY. Copyright © 2006 by Jared Fogle. All rights reserved. Printed in the United States of America. No part of this book may be used or reproduced in any manner whatsoever without written permission except in the case of brief quotations embodied in critical articles or reviews. For information, address St. Martin's Press, 175 Fifth Avenue, New York, N.Y. 10010.

www.stmartins.com

Library of Congress Cataloging-in-Publication Data

Fogle, Jared.
    Jared, the Subway guy : winning through losing : 13 lessons for turning your life around / Jared Fogle, Anthony Bruno.—1st ed.
        p.   cm.
    ISBN-13: 978-0-312-35358-2
    ISBN-10: 0-312-35358-8
    1. Weight loss.   2. Self-care, health.   3. Nutrition.   4. Dieters.   I. Bruno, Anthony.   II. Title.

RM222.2F637   2006
613.2'5—dc22   2006043897

First Edition: August 2006

10 9 8 7 6 5 4 3 2 1

To all the people in the world who are overcoming obstacles in their lives, and to all those who desperately want to

Contents

Acknowledgments

I would like to thank JL Lou for his incredible kindness and compassion in helping me face my weight problem and overcome it. JL was always there for me during my most difficult times. If it weren't for his honesty and his friendship, I probably wouldn't be alive today.

I also want to thank Ryan Coleman for writing the newspaper article that eventually brought me to national attention. None of the great things that have happened to me would have ever occurred if it weren't for Ryan.

Praise and thanks to Mike Mead, my manager, whose tireless efforts have helped to bring my message to a larger audience.

Over the years Subway and their family of franchisees have always made me feel special. I consider myself extremely fortunate to have their constant, enthusiastic support.

I'm very grateful for my ongoing relationship with the MMB Agency. They have consistently presented me and my story with both creativity and honesty.

I would also like to thank my editor at St. Martin's Press, Elizabeth Beier; my literary agent, Al Zuckerman of Writers House; and author Anthony Bruno, who helped me write this book.

Introduction

This is not a diet book. Diet books are about losing.

This is a book about gaining. Gaining knowledge. Gaining confidence. Gaining self-esteem. Gaining happiness. It's about getting healthy, both physically and mentally. It's about knocking down the obstacles that stand in your way and putting them behind you. In other words, this book is about getting a life.

I got my life back when I dropped 245 pounds. You can get yours back, too, no matter what obstacles you face. Trust me.

This book is not just for people with weight issues. Problems are problems. Phobias, extreme shyness, addiction to drugs, alcohol, nicotine, shopping, gambling—they're all obstacles in your way, stones on the road. Most of us make these stones immovable boulders through our own ingrained dumb habits. That's what I did. When I was at my heaviest, I was eating more than 10,000 calories a day—burgers, fries, shakes, chips, pizzas, fried chicken, tacos, you name it. A normal person my height should eat about 2,000 calories a day. I couldn't imagine how I could ever cut down to that.

But I wasn't ignorant of the dangers. I knew I was harming myself. I knew what healthy eating was all about because my father is a doctor. He'd told me about eating balanced meals and taking it easy on fatty, high-calorie foods—all the things I loved. My mother prepared healthy, satisfying meals every day. And yet I still pigged out.

I overate to compensate for my social awkwardness. I overate because I spent way too much time sitting around playing video games and watching TV. I overate because I just plain loved the taste of food. But as I grew fatter and fatter, I felt more isolated. Eventually I felt that I didn't have any real friends in the world except for one. Food.

A lot of people know who I am because of the Subway sandwich shop commercials. I'm well known for holding up my "fat pants," a pair of my old jeans with a 60-inch waist. I've appeared in more than thirty Subway commercials that have been shown across the country and overseas as well. I've been on countless television shows, including *Oprah,* and I was featured as a cartoon character in an episode of *South Park*. On more than a few occasions I've been the punch line to jokes told by late-night talk show hosts. I got famous because I was once tremendously obese, and then, after losing an incredible amount of weight, I wasn't.

But I'm cool with that because the recognition I've acquired has given me the opportunity to work with the American Heart Association, leading Heart Walks to raise awareness about healthy choices and heart disease. My fame has also given me the opportunity to speak out about childhood obesity, a topic I know quite a bit about from personal experience. Most important, it has allowed me to give other people hope, people with all kinds of problems, not just weight issues.

I believe that all of us can change our lives. I did, and you can, too.

I have to repeat, this is not a diet book. I've read a ton of diet books, and none of them helped me. It's not that they were all worthless. Some people have lost weight following the advice in those books and the programs they recommend. But I can say with confidence that no matter what you're trying to accomplish, **you'll never get anywhere until you yourself are ready, and you decide you're going to do it no matter what.**

For twelve years I suffered with my expanding body, and during all that time I kept on eating because I wasn't ready to do anything about it. Sure, I told myself I was ready to buckle down and change my habits, but deep down I wasn't prepared to give up midnight pizza snacks or Big Macs or Whoppers or buckets of Kentucky Fried Chicken or Big Gulps or any of that. I wasn't ready to change.

But when I finally decided it was time to get serious—truly serious—I got my butt in gear (a huge effort for me) and did something about it. My plan was almost ridiculously simple, but I stuck to it and I made it work. Through trial and error, I got myself mentally prepared, settled on a diet that made sense to me, and followed through on it.

As I shed pounds, I learned some important lessons, lessons that *you* can apply to remove any boulder standing in your path. I didn't even know they were lessons until I looked back and took account of what I had done. My hope is that you can learn from these same lessons. Right now you're probably using a useless little tack hammer to chip away at your immense problem. Well, let me give you a great big bulldozer.

The solution you come up with—and *you* will have to be the one who comes up with it—won't be easy, and the results won't come instantly. But it will make sense to you because it will be yours. And that's why it will work.

When I peaked at 425 pounds as a freshman at Indiana University, I was literally the boulder on my own road. Over an eleven-month period, I melted that boulder down to 180 pounds. I gained back 10 and leveled off at 190, and I've maintained that weight for the past six years. And I'm a very happy camper, because I got my life back.

My story will show you what I learned from my struggle with obesity and give you hope and real help that you can apply to any problem you may have. I want you to get your life back, too.

JARED, THE SUBWAY GUY

LESSON 1

Open Your Eyes

The first step toward change is recognizing that you have a problem. When I was at my heaviest, every time I passed a mirror, every morning when I got dressed, every time I had to haul myself out of a chair—nearly everything I did told me that I had a serious weight problem. *But I refused to acknowledge it.*

Simply admitting that you have a problem is a *huge* step. In the beginning you don't even have to do anything about the problem. Just think about it. Consider your situation objectively and try to see it for what it is. All you have to do is admit that you have a problem and you're already on the road to a solution.

I will never forget the day I went to my endocrinologist's office to finally face the music. It was the scariest day of my life. Just being in the examining room made me panicky and claustrophobic even though it was bigger than the little rooms you find in a regular doctor's office. The table was larger and closer to the ground. The chairs were extra wide with no armrests. The blood pressure cuff hanging on the wall was big enough to put around some people's waists. And then there was the scale.

I remember sitting on the table, staring at the scale as I waited for the nurse to come in and weigh me. This was the moment I had been dreading for years. I had put off this examination for as long as I could, even tried to figure out ways to cancel the appointment by faking some sort of mysterious illness that would save me from this monster embarrassment. But the scale was right there, standing against the wall, looking back at me, waiting for me to get on, snickering as if it already knew how much I weighed.

I knew this had to be done. Not so much for my health—I wasn't even thinking about that. I just wanted to save myself from further embarrassment. I knew that doctors' scales—even the superheavyweight models—went up only to a certain weight. The one in my father's office topped out at 350. I had no idea how much weight this one could handle, but I did know that if you maxed out on one of these babies, you had only two alternatives. I'd either have to go down to the local meat-packing plant and get weighed on the scales they use for livestock, or I could drive to a truck stop with a weigh station where they'd weigh my car with me in it, then weigh it again with me not in it, subtracting one figure from the other to get my weight. In either case people would be watching, and I didn't want to be gawked at like a side of beef or a big rig.

But more than that, I just didn't want to know. I was in

denial. I knew I had a problem, but somehow not knowing the specifics seemed better than having to face a cold, hard, undeniable number.

The examining room was silent except for the muffled sound of easy-listening music filtering in from the waiting room. I wondered if they played this kind of bland, soothing music for the steers before they went to slaughter.

The room had no windows, and now I really started to feel closed in. The office was on the ground floor of the building, and I wondered if there was a back door. There had to be, I thought. I could sneak down the hall and slip out the back. But then I thought about it. At my size I didn't do much sneaking or slipping out of anything. Wherever I was, my body made a statement—even (or should I say, especially) when I didn't want to.

I drummed my fingers on the edge of the table. My mouth was dry. I cracked my knuckles out of nervousness. My legs trembled. I was afraid that if I tried to stand up, my knees would buckle. Then I'd be on the floor, and believe me, getting back up wouldn't be easy.

I realized that there was no escape, no way around it, no talking my way out of it.

This was my vision of *hell,* and I was scared.

Suddenly I heard a knock on the door. It was a light, fast knock—one, two, three—but to my ears it was a battering ram breaking down the door. The Fat Police were here to get me. I was busted!

"May I come in, Jared?" It was the nurse who'd brought me back to this room. She sounded so nice, like someone's mother.

I didn't answer. I couldn't.

"Jared?" she said. "Are you all right?"

I coughed. "Ah . . . yeah," I said. "I'm fine."

"May I come in?"

Could I say no? Was that an option? And what if I did? Would she get the doctor? Would she get my father, who was waiting in the reception area? Please no, I thought. I didn't want anyone else to see me on the scale.

"Yeah, sure," I said. "You can come in."

The door opened, and there she was, a nice middle-aged lady with wire-rimmed glasses, short blond hair, and a kind smile. Too young to be a grandmother but too old to have kids still in school, kind of that in-between age. She was wearing pale blue scrubs and a stethoscope hung around her neck. She seemed totally nice, but there was one thing about her that made me wary. She was carrying a clipboard. My chart was on that clipboard. The chart where she wanted to write down my weight.

"Can you step up on the scale for me, Jared?"

I didn't know what to do.

"You don't have to take your shoes off," she said.

Obviously the extra weight of a pair of sneakers didn't matter much at my size, but she was probably trying to spare me the ordeal of having to bend over and put them back on later.

She stood by and waited patiently as I slowly got off the table and stood up. My knees felt so weak I was afraid to take a step, fearing that I might collapse on the floor. Then what would they do? Call a tow truck?

I moved carefully, taking sliding baby steps toward the scale. I could swear the damn thing was laughing at me.

"Just step right up on there," the nurse said. "That's it."

My brain was telling me not to do it: *Faint if you have to, Jared.* But I did as she asked. I knew there was no way out of it.

The counterweights were already pushed to the left and set at zero. The scale clanked as I stepped onto it, and the pointer clunked into the up position. Sweat was dripping down my brow. I usually perspired a lot because of my weight, but this was beyond normal. This was panic sweat.

"Okay," the nurse said. "Let's see how we do."

She slid the big counterweight to the right, past the 100-, 150-, 200-, and 250-pound notches, stopping at 300.

The pointer didn't budge.

She slid the small counterweight to the right, nudging it along.

I forced myself to keep my eyes open, staring at the pointer. It wasn't moving.

She got to the midway point.

Nothing.

She nudged the counterweight faster until she moved it all the way to the right.

The pointer didn't move.

Oh, God, I thought. I was over 350. I had kind of suspected that I was, but how much over 350?

She slid the small counterweight back to the left and moved the big one over another notch to 350. She slowly moved the small weight to the right.

The pointer stayed right where it was. I started to wonder if it was glued there and this was some kind of sick joke.

She kept pushing the small weight with her finger. I stopped breathing, waiting for the pointer to move. 360 . . . 370 . . . 380 . . . 390 . . . 395 . . .

She slid the small weight back to the left and reached for the big weight. My mouth was a desert.

"Do you want me to take my shoes off?" I asked. I sounded so lame.

"That's okay," she said, maintaining her pleasant demeanor. Whatever she thought of me and my monstrous size, she wasn't letting on.

She put her finger on the big weight and pushed it over another notch to the 400-pound position. My heart was slamming in my chest. She started to nudge the small weight. 405 . . . 410 . . . The pointer didn't move, not even a flutter.

She kept pushing.

I closed my eyes. I couldn't look.

My shirt was drenched. I wanted an earthquake to crack open the earth and swallow me up. I wanted to disappear. I didn't want to be here.

The sound of the metal weight sliding along the metal bar was like a samurai sword slowly sinking into my chest. When was it going to stop? I thought. *When?*

I wasn't born fat. As a little kid, I was pretty normal, and I played all kinds of sports—basketball, baseball, soccer, tennis; I even ran track. But when I started third grade, something happened and little by little I started to gain weight.

One contributing factor I can pinpoint is that I just loved food. All kinds of food. Healthy food, not-so-healthy food, junk food—you name it, I liked it. Everyone in my family loved food. Our kitchen was always well stocked—mostly with healthy food (my father was a physician, after all), but my mother kept some junk food around, like chips and soda, for occasional treats. But while everyone in my immediate family and even my extended family loved food, I was the only one who gained a ton of weight. Somehow everyone else managed to burn off the calories better than I did.

Looking back, maybe I loved food a little bit more than they did. I recently found my fourth grade journal and was shocked to find that nearly every entry was about food. That's all I wrote about. I would go on and on about food, particularly school lunches. Every kid I knew thought cafeteria food was the worst, but not me. I *loved* cafeteria food. I looked forward to it. If a breeze blew into the classroom from the cafeteria and I got a whiff of what was on the menu that day, I was like that cartoon dog who floats on air, totally blissed out by the mere thought of getting a dog biscuit.

I loved cafeteria food so much I would eat my friends' leftovers. I was particularly fond of the hamburgers—the steamed bun, the machine-made grilled patty, the glob of ketchup—and whenever I could, I would sneak an extra dollar to school so I could buy an extra burger.

The other factor that contributed to my weight gain was my social awkwardness. When I was little, I didn't dwell on rejection or hurt feelings. If I was ever sad about something, the feeling didn't last very long, and I bounced back pretty quickly. But by the time I entered the fourth grade, slights and insults became big things. I felt that I didn't fit in very well, and now that I was getting chubby, I felt even more isolated. I thought that no one liked me and there was nothing I could do to improve the situation. So in the tilted logic of a self-conscious fat kid, food became my only friend.

If I wasn't picked to play in a basketball game, I bought myself a package of Twinkies.

If a popular kid snubbed me on the playground, I went home after school and made myself a sundae.

If I overheard kids making jokes about my size, my next stop was McDonald's.

Food never disappointed me the way other kids did. It always tasted good. It didn't talk about me behind my back or make fun of me or criticize me. It was always there for me the way a true-blue friend should be. It gave me love and comfort whenever I needed it. Of course, fat-kid logic prevented me from realizing that the larger I got the more out of place I felt. I just couldn't make that connection.

Even though I was sensitive about my weight, I could still take a joke if it wasn't mean-spirited. In fact, my father was always quick with a joke, and occasionally he'd make one about my weight. He certainly didn't mean to be hurtful, but everyone and everything was fair game for his brand of humor, and our whole family accepted that. One summer when I was in middle school, my family went on a trip to the Grand Canyon. We all had a great time, and of course we took a lot of pictures. A few days after we got home, my mom brought home the developed photos, and we all sat around the kitchen table before dinner going through them. One shot sticks out in my mind—me sitting on a donkey. The donkey doesn't look happy and actually seems to be making a face.

The day that photo was taken we were on a trail ride down into the canyon. My dad had asked the guide to find a donkey strong enough to accommodate me, and he jokingly asked if there'd be an extra charge if I broke the donkey's back. Everybody got a good laugh out of that, even me. I knew he loved me and that it was just one of his little jokes. At the time I equated my size with strength and power. I mean, did anyone ever call the Hulk fat? Or the Thing? I don't think so.

But the photo didn't show the Jared I had imagined myself to be. I definitely didn't look like a superhero on a charging steed. I looked like a pathetic fat kid on a really ticked-off donkey, and in hindsight my father's comment to the guide that day hurt more than my father could ever have imagined.

After seeing that photo, whenever kids at school made me the butt of their jokes, I cringed and withdrew. It sent me back into my shell. And whenever I retreated from the world, you know who I turned to.

• • •

By fifth grade, I was sneaking food so that my parents wouldn't know I was overeating. I remember one time when my parents let me stay home alone. They'd told me the week before that they'd be going out for the evening and that my brother and sister would be staying over with friends, which meant I had time to plan. I couldn't wait for that night to come.

I watched from the front window and waved good-bye to them as their car backed out of the driveway. I'd told them to have a good time and not to worry, I'd be fine. But inside I was so giddy and excited I could have exploded. My plan was to call out for a pizza and have it delivered. A large Pizza Hut Meat Lover's pizza with sausage, pepperoni, hamburger, and extra cheese. For days I had been thinking about this pizza. It would be all mine. It would be like an old friend coming over for a visit. I must have been salivating on the windowsill, I was so delirious.

I waited ten whole minutes to make sure my parents were really gone and wouldn't be coming back because they'd forgotten something. Then I ran to the phone and ordered my dream pizza.

"It'll be there in twenty-five minutes," the man on the other end said.

"Great," I said.

And it was great. I remember sitting in the living room by the front window, waiting for the delivery truck, thinking this was the happiest day of my life. Me alone with a large pizza was my version of paradise.

I pulled the crumpled-up dollar bills I'd saved out of my

jeans and smoothed them out on my thigh. I didn't dare go watch TV or play Nintendo while I waited. What if I didn't hear the doorbell and missed my pizza? I couldn't imagine what I'd do. So I sat in the armchair facing the window and waited.

When headlights swept the front of the house, I leaped out of my seat. I went to the window. The pizza truck was pulling into the driveway. A college kid got out and started walking to the front door with a thermal pizza case in his hands.

I ran to the door and opened it before he had a chance to ring the bell.

"Fogle?" the college kid asked. "Large Meat Lover's with extra cheese?"

I think I managed to say yes, but I might have been too intoxicated by the aroma of the hot pizza to form a full sentence. I handed him the money—I'd already figured out how much it would be and added a generous tip. I certainly didn't want him coming back the next time my parents ordered pizza, complaining about the lousy tip he'd gotten the last time he was here. No, I had thought this through completely, and I intended to cover all my tracks.

The college kid handed me the pizza. "Have a good night," he said before he trotted back to his truck.

"I will," I called after him.

I closed the door and headed to the kitchen with my prize, setting it down carefully on the table. I opened the lid. Steam wafted to the ceiling and fogged my glasses. The smell was incredible. I couldn't believe it. This was a dream come true. Alone with a pizza all to myself.

I picked out the little plastic table in the middle of the pizza that kept the cheese from sticking to the lid of the box and tossed it on the counter. I separated my first slice, raised it to my mouth, and bit into it. It was heavy with toppings and so hot it burned the roof of my mouth. But I didn't care. This was *my* pizza.

I finished the first slice and went on to the second. Then the third and the fourth and the fifth and the sixth and the seventh and finally the eighth. I ate so fast the last piece was still warm as I ate it. In a few short minutes I had demolished the entire pizza. And now I felt awful.

I was stuffed. I had eaten too fast and was beginning to feel sick. But my physical discomfort was nothing compared to my fear that my parents would suddenly walk in the door and find out what I'd just done. I had to stick to my original plan, I told myself. I had to cover my tracks.

The first thing I did was fold the empty pizza box as tight as I could and step on it to flatten it even further; then I buried it in the trash can, covering it with stuff that was already in there.

Next, I found a can of air freshener under the sink and sprayed the room until it smelled like a flower shop instead of a pizza parlor.

Finally I went to the refrigerator and took out one of the frozen dinners I had told my parents I was going to be eating. I quickly microwaved it, then scraped the food into the garbage disposal to get rid of it. I left the dirty plastic tray on the counter so that it would look as if I had eaten that for dinner. I looked around the room and gave it the once-over. When I was satisfied that there was no evidence of a pizza ever having been there, I went downstairs to veg out in front of the TV and let my stomach settle, confident that I had covered my tracks completely.

I would later find out, however, that I was no criminal mastermind. (How many ten-year-old boys are?) My parents returned a little after ten o'clock, and within five minutes I was busted.

"Jared?" my mother called to me from the kitchen. I could tell by her high-pitched tone that something was up.

I walked into the kitchen. Both my parents were there waiting for me. They looked grim.

"What's this?" my mother said. She was holding the little plastic pizza table in her palm, like a giant about to crush it.

Oops. I'd tossed it on the counter and forgotten about it. How stupid!

"Catching up on your reading?" my father said, pointing to the yellow pages on the counter under the wall phone. It was open to the "Pizza" listings.

Oops again. My face felt hot. I looked at my reflection in the chrome toaster. My face was as red as pizza sauce.

My mom stepped on the garbage pail pedal, and the lid popped open. She picked around in the trash a bit and found the folded pizza box. I guess I hadn't buried it as deeply as I'd thought. Oops number three.

I felt soooo stupid. And embarrassed. Now I had to own up to it, which wasn't easy for me. For me a pizza wasn't just a pizza. It was something I coveted, so now I had to admit to my guilty pleasure.

I was grounded for two weeks. My father told me I had

to come straight home after school every day and a sleep-over scheduled for the next weekend at my house was go-ing to be canceled. My parents lectured me big-time that night, the first of many lectures. They had concrete proof that I was sneaking food, and they got on me about it be-cause they were concerned about me. But the more they lectured me, the more ashamed and resentful I became. In-stead of learning my lesson, I resolved to get sneakier and hide my traces better. My parents didn't realize it, but they were actually pushing me toward the only friend I could depend on for uncritical comfort—food.

Whenever I felt down, I'd hop on my bike and sneak over to "fast-food row," which unfortunately was just a convenient five minutes from my house. McDonald's, Burger King, Dunkin' Donuts, Wendy's, Taco Bell, Roy Rogers, KFC—we had them all. It was so comforting to see their bright lights shining in the distance as I pedaled toward them. I was going to be with my friends.

Another major turning point in my relationship with food came in the sixth grade, when I graduated to middle school. In elementary school I had always looked forward to lunch in the cafeteria. Every day I would go through the line, pick up my meal, carry my tray to my seat, and chow down. Seats were assigned in the cafeteria so there was never an issue as to where I would sit or who'd be next to me.

But in middle school all that changed. Kids could sit wherever they wanted in the cafeteria, and for me it was a social bazaar full of cliques and gangs and perplexing alliances. There were tables for the jocks and tables for the cool kids, tables for the brains and tables for the artsy kids. There was even a table for the misfits. But there wasn't a table for fat kids like me.

In middle school I felt conspicuous because of my weight. I would never dream of getting on a scale, but I must have been somewhere in the low 200s. All I really wanted to do was disappear and become invisible. Initially I tried sitting with the misfits—the Trekkers, the goths, the weird kids who lived in their own worlds—but eventually they bonded with one another and formed their own group that didn't include me. They'd laugh and joke and horse around, and I was right there, but none of them would talk to me. They made it obvious that I wasn't part of their circle. I was just taking up space at their table.

Eventually I stopped sitting with them and instead sat at a small table all by myself. If you've ever watched an over-weight person eating by himself, you know that it's a sad sight. The fat person doesn't enjoy his meal. He feels guilty and isolated. He doesn't want to be alone, but he also doesn't want people to see him eat. He fears being criticized or mocked.

The emotional pain of being obese is truly debilitating. It was for me. It sent me deeper into my shell and encouraged more sneak-eating. It was the only comfort I had. By seventh grade I avoided as many school activities as I could get away with. I stopped playing sports. I quit playing tennis and taking lessons, the one sport I really liked. Of course, that just made things worse. Without exercise I got heavier, and the heavier I got, the more I withdrew into myself.

By this time my sedentary lifestyle was taking its toll. My back always hurt. My shoulders would crack, and my ankles would pop for no apparent reason. I would get winded easily, and occasionally my knees would buckle.

I was plagued with the Curse of Obesity, which clouded my thinking. What makes perfect sense to everyone else in the world doesn't compute for a seriously overweight person.

"Find a good diet and stick to it," people would tell me.

"Do some exercise."

"Just shut your mouth."

Pretty logical, right?

Well, not if you have the Curse. The Curse nullifies logic. It puts obstacles in your way that only you can see. Worst of all, it makes you *afraid*—afraid of rejection and afraid of failure.

It's the same with a person suffering from anorexia. "Just eat, why don't you?" people say.

"Just stop drinking," people tell alcoholics.

"Don't take drugs anymore," they tell addicts.

But it's not that simple. There are complex factors involved with these addictions, psychological issues that must be dealt with first, and most reasonably intelligent people understand that.

Except when it comes to people who have a weight problem. Somehow most people think of obesity as a lesser addiction, perhaps because so many suffer from it. You have to give up alcohol or drugs completely to break those addictions. But you must keep eating every day in order to live.

Think about it. When was the last time you saw someone sniffing glue in public? Or snorting cocaine? That would be shocking, and you'd probably pity that person for succumbing to his addiction so blatantly.

But when was the last time you saw a fat person eating? Not so shocking or unusual.

But you probably don't pity that person or try to understand his or her problem. If anything you probably cluck your tongue at their weakness as if they could stop at any time if they really wanted to. And it's that dismissive condemnation that makes people with the Curse eat more. That's the Curse of Obesity.

When I got to high school, kids asked me why I wasn't going out for the football team. Everyone thought I would be a natural playing on the line. I'd just laugh and give them my standard response. "Sure," I'd say, "but if I get knocked down, I don't think I'd get back up." I'd make a joke about it, but on the inside I wasn't laughing. One of my greatest fears was that I'd fall down and really injure myself. I dreaded the winter months. Not because of the cold. I was never cold. I was always sweating, because of my weight. It was the ice on the ground that I feared. My balance was precarious enough on dry pavement. I had nightmares about slipping on the ice and putting my back out of commission for good.

High school was a lonely time for me. I knew a lot of kids, but I didn't really consider any of them my friends, except for JL. We sort of found one another because we were both outsiders—me because of my weight and him because he had emigrated from China to the United States when he was thirteen. He often didn't understand American culture, and the habits of American teenagers frequently baffled him.

One evening I happened to run into him at the movies. We were in the same English class, and the assignment for that week was to see the film *The Madness of King George*. We ended up sitting together, and afterward I asked him if he'd like to join me for a snack at the Country Buffet.

"What did you think of the movie?" he asked me as we went through the buffet line.

"It was okay," I said. Frankly my mind was on the assortment of foods spread out in front of me. It all looked so good, I didn't know where to start.

"Do you think it was really historically accurate?" JL asked.

"I don't know," I said. "Hard to say." I was shaking a serving spoon over my plate, trying to get a glob of potato salad unstuck.

"You can't always trust a movie to be true to history," JL said as he went directly to the salad bar.

"That's true," I said.

While JL made himself a salad, I loaded up my plate. Rolls of cold cuts—ham, roast beef, Swiss cheese. I took a couple of stuffed peppers. A slab of veal parmesan. Pork chops with apple sauce. A dripping mound of creamy cole slaw because I figured I needed a vegetable. Finally I filled two tall glasses with Coke and wandered over to the table that JL had found for us.

He'd already started eating, and as I took my seat, I

thought it was strange that he hadn't taken more food. All he had on his tray was a small salad, a tuna-fish sandwich, and an iced tea. It didn't even look like he'd put dressing on his salad, certainly not a creamy one.

"So what do you think Mr. Wade will ask us about the movie?" JL said, referring to our English teacher.

"I'm not sure," I said. But I wasn't thinking about the movie. I was thinking about food, a little embarrassed by the huge mound of stuff I had on my plate compared to what JL had on his.

But JL didn't say anything about it. He wasn't judgmental that way. He accepted me for who I was and I accepted him for who he was, and that's why we got along. We just kind of understood one another.

I didn't participate in any extracurricular activities in high school, except for the Junior Historical Society, which wasn't exactly where the popular kids hung out. I didn't go to dances or football games or anything like that. Occasionally after school I would have to help with a group project for class, but that was mandatory. Otherwise, as soon as the 3:00 P.M. bell rang, I was out the door. I'd go straight back home to my video games, my TV, and my refrigerator—the friends who never disappointed me.

By senior year I figured I must have broken the 300-pound mark, but by how much I had no idea, and I had no intention of finding out. It wasn't crucial information as far as I was concerned. But then came the day when we had to order our caps and gowns for graduation. And anything to do with clothing was a humiliating situation.

A representative from the company that rented the caps and gowns had set up shop in a corner of the cafeteria. The young woman was scheduled to be there for the entire day, and all seniors had to go fill out an order form and let her take measurements. Just what I did not want to do.

But I did want to graduate with my class, and I didn't want to disappoint my family by not going to the ceremony, so I gritted my teeth and went down to the cafeteria to take care of the cap and gown order. I picked up an order form and got in line. The form asked for name, address, phone number, height, weight, waist size, neck size, and head size. I looked past the kids in front of me and saw that the rep had a tailor's tape measure hanging around her neck. She was mostly taking head measurements but also some waist and neck measurements from the kids who didn't have a clue about their sizes. I considered turning around and walking out, but then I noticed that most of the girls were filling in the embarrassing information before they got to the rep, so I pulled out a pen and did the same.

I wrote down 304 for my weight, picking a number that I thought sounded realistic. I knew I was 6'2", so I wrote that down for my height. The jeans my mom usually bought for me had a 52-inch waist so I wrote that down. As for my neck size, I had no idea. I hadn't bought a dress shirt in years, and the last time I did, I thought it was something like an 18-inch neck. I added two more inches and wrote down "20."

I moved up in line and finally got to the cap-and-gown lady. I handed her the form and hoped to God she wouldn't try using that tape measure on me, especially on my waist.

What if her tape wasn't long enough? How would she measure me? She was a small woman. How would she even get her arms around me? Would she have to call for help? How embarrassing would that be?

My pulse was racing as she scanned the form. I was praying for mercy.

She looked up from the form and must have seen the distress in my eyes. "All I need is your head measurement, Jared," she said with a smile.

I bent forward and let her wrap the tape around my head, hoping that it would end here.

She jotted down the measurement and hung the tape around her neck.

"Okay," she said, "you're all set."

I assumed she was experienced in dealing with fat kids, and I was incredibly grateful for that. I walked back to class, feeling that for once I had dodged a bullet.

Unfortunately I hadn't. It was just a delayed bullet.

A few days later I got a phone call at home. My sister answered it.

"Jared, it's for you," she said, yelling down to the rec room, where I was playing video games.

I picked up the downstairs extension. "Hello?"

"Hi," the man on the other end said. "Is this Jared Fogle?"

"Yes."

"Jared, I'm from Scholar's Choice. The cap and gown company?"

"Yes?" I could feel it coming.

"We've reviewed your form, and if this information is

correct, I'm afraid we're going to have to special order a cap and gown for you. Would you like to go over the measurements with me to make sure what I have is accurate?"

"No," I said.

"Oh . . . okay. I have to tell you, though, for special orders, we have to charge a little extra."

"Fine," I said. "Whatever." I didn't care. I did not want to deal with this.

"It's thirty-five dollars on top of the regular charge. Do you want to check with your parents first?"

"No. It's fine. Just send us a bill."

"Okay, we can do that. I'll put the order in today, so you'll have it in time for graduation."

"Great."

"Thanks for your business, Jared. Bye now."

"Bye."

I hung up the phone. My face was on fire. I could feel the sweat pouring down my sides under my shirt.

I heard his voice in my head. *Thanks for being a blimp, Jared.*

"Yeah, thanks a lot," I grumbled under my breath.

I reached over to the open bag of corn chips on the end table next to me and grabbed a fistful. I stuffed my mouth and chomped down, closing my eyes and letting the crunch of the chips block out all sound. I did not want to deal with this, not any of it.

"Jared? Jared? You can step down now."

I opened my eyes and blinked. I was standing on the scale in the endocrinologist's office. I'd forgotten where I was for a moment. The nurse was next to me, smiling kindly, the chart down by her side. I immediately zoned in on the pointer. It was floating at midpoint. I looked at the counterweights.

It said 425.

I couldn't believe it.

425!

The nurse slid the counterweights back to zero.

425? I thought. It can't be.

My knees were shaking. I wanted to cry. This couldn't be.

"Have a seat on the table, Jared," the nurse said. "I'm just going to take some blood samples. Then the doctor will be in to see you."

Open Your Eyes

- As the saying goes, "Denial ain't just a river in Egypt." If you want to change your life, you have to face reality first. Take a good hard look in the mirror and admit that you have a problem.

- In the beginning, don't try to do anything about your problem. Just admit that the problem exists.

- Whatever your addiction is—food, drugs, alcohol, tobacco, spending, whatever—it is *not* your friend. For a long time you have turned to it for consolation and comfort, but it has not helped you in the past and it will not help you in the future.

- Your problem might seem enormous and impossible to overcome, and that fills you with fear and anxiety. You're afraid to risk failure. You feel that if you fail, the people you know will reject you. Well, get over it. No one is watching your situation as closely as you are. If you're not willing to risk failure, you will never succeed.

Do Something

Finding a solution to any major problem is like buying a new pair of shoes. You have to try on a few pairs, or maybe more than a few pairs, to find the right fit. No matter what bad habit you're trying to kick, you might have to try several different approaches before you find the one that's right for you. *But you have to risk failure and try **something***. If it doesn't work, you can always move on to something else, the same way you can ask the shoe-store clerk for another pair of shoes to try on.

When you're stuck in a rut and your problem is getting the better of you, *do something, anything,* to create some momentum. In all likelihood you won't hit a bull's-eye on your first try, but at least you'll be moving in the right direction.

I tried several different diets before I found the one that worked for me, but before I got to the point where I would even consider trying a diet, I had to be scared into action. My endocrinologist took care of that.

As I sat on the examining table in his office, waiting for him to come in, I was already nervous, dreading what he would tell me. I jumped when I heard the doorknob turning.

"Hello, Jared," he said as he pulled my chart out of rack on the outside of the door.

"Hi," I said. My mouth was bone-dry.

The doctor was an average-looking middle-aged guy, but he was scaring the hell out of me, and he hadn't even said anything yet. As he examined my chart, I watched his face, looking for signs of shock or disapproval, but he was hard to read. He listened to my heart and lungs with his stethoscope and felt the glands in my neck. My nerves jangled as he proceeded with his examination, and my heart was stuck in my throat. I was terrified of what he might tell me.

He took a seat on a stool and jotted down some notes on my chart. When he was through, he took off his glasses and put them in his shirt pocket.

Oh, God! I thought. Here it comes!

"Jared," he said, "you're facing some significant health risks carrying this much weight. You know that, don't you?"

"Yeah." My breathing was shallow, my heart pounding.

"You're putting yourself at risk for type 2 diabetes."

"You mean I have diabetes?" I asked in a panic.

"I can't answer that question right now. We'll have to wait for your tests to come back. But that's not the only thing. Morbid obesity puts you at risk for hypertension."

Morbid obesity. I knew the phrase, but I'd never actually heard anyone use it in reference to me. It made me feel as if I could drop dead at any moment.

"And," the doctor said, "if your cholesterol levels are elevated—as I suspect they are—you're at risk for heart disease."

"You mean, I could have a heart attack? But I'm only twenty years old."

The doctor nodded gravely. "Young people have can heart attacks, too. It happens."

Oh, my God, I thought. Why don't we just go straight to the funeral parlor and fit me for a coffin? But did they make coffins in my size? I wondered.

"Obesity has also been connected to the onset of certain types of cancer later in life," he said.

I was feeling faint.

"And then there's sleep apnea," the doctor continued, "which is a condition in which you stop breathing while you sleep. Do you snore?"

"Yeah . . . I think."

The doctor nodded. "I'm not saying you have apnea, but snoring is a symptom."

"I don't know, maybe I don't snore," I said. "I'm not sure." I was desperate to minimize the gravity of the situation.

"Jared, I want you to go on a diet." He held out a booklet to me.

My hands must have been trembling as I took it. I had a feeling that this was coming. I stared at the booklet as if it were a foreign object, something that had dropped out of the sky from outer space. I knew more than a little about these kinds of diets because my father kept similar booklets at his office and I'd looked through them in the past.

"I know you're away at college, Jared, but I strongly advise you to follow this diet. You're a young man and your health is at risk, but the situation can be reversed. But only if you're willing to do what it takes."

"I'll try," I said.

But inside I had no intention of trying. I just wanted to get the hell out of there.

"I know you can do it," the doctor said with a reassuring smile. "My nurse will give you a call when your tests come in to let you know if we need an immediate follow-up. In the meantime . . ." He pointed to the booklet in my hand. "Good luck." He shook my hand. "You can get dressed now." He whisked out the door to take care of his next patient.

My head was spinning as I trudged back out to the waiting room. I was up to my eyeballs in all kinds of information and warnings, but the only thing I could focus on was that number: 425! How did I get to this point? Being a little over 300 pounds in high school seemed manageable by comparison. (Fat logic again.) It wasn't that far from the 200s, and the low 200s would almost be a healthy weight for my height, so I was still within striking distance of being normal, I had felt.

But being over 400 put me into a whole different category. That was sideshow-freak weight, I thought. Over 400 was beyond striking distance to normal. That was two times normal. No matter how I wrestled with the numbers, it always came out bad. Mortally bad.

The numbers game is something that all people with serious problems play. You work the numbers in your head, trying to find a formula that doesn't make the situation seem as bad as it really is. Whether it's pounds or alcoholic drinks or joints or money lost in poker games, you can always twist the numbers until they seem less drastic than they really are.

"There are only six drinks in a pitcher of margaritas. I ordered two pitchers, but my friend had a couple, and I was at the bar for five hours. So if you figure it out, I really didn't drink that much."

"I only smoke marijuana at night, and just enough to get buzzed. It's good for stress management. And an ounce lasts me forever. So I'm really not getting that high."

"Yeah, I lost a lot of money playing poker tonight, but if I keep playing, the odds will be with me. All I have to do is win 60 percent of the time for the next two nights and I'll break even. And, hey, what's 60 percent? That's nothing."

See what I mean?

My father tried to make conversation as we drove home from the endocrinologist's office, but I wasn't very communicative. I was driving.

"Do you have any questions about anything the doctor told you?" he asked me.

"Nope," I said. "He explained it pretty well."

I had all that bad news crammed into my head, and I was frantically working the numbers, furiously trying to make them better than they were. Except at 425 pounds, I was having a hard time making a purse out of this sow's ear. There was no getting around it. I had a serious problem.

But knowing that I had a problem didn't smarten me up any.

I drove home and dropped off my father.

"Aren't you coming in?" he asked.

"No, I thought I'd go down to the library and look up some stuff."

"Okay." My dad could see how glum I was, and he probably figured I was going to look up information about the risks of obesity and check out various diet books. Well, that was the impression I wanted him to have because I had no intention of going to the library. I needed to find someone I could commiserate with, someone who would make me feel better. I needed to see my old friend Denny.

That's right. I drove to the local Denny's restaurant, squeezed myself into a booth, and ordered the "Lumberjack Slam"—three eggs, bacon, sausage, ham, hash browns, toast, and a stack of pancakes. I washed it all down with a chocolate milk shake. After all, I told myself, I needed the calcium from the milk and ice cream. I ate the whole thing, every last bite, and as I mopped the last morsel of pancake in maple syrup, I thought to myself, *I'll start dieting tomorrow*.

In the back of my mind I kept thinking—no, *hoping*—that what I really had was a glandular problem and that the results of my blood tests would show that. The endocrinologist would then prescribe a pill that would magically reduce me back to normal size in no time.

Well, dream on, Jared.

The endocrinologist's nurse called a few days later to tell me that my blood tests had come back. There was nothing wrong with my glands, she said, which meant there wasn't going to be a magic-pill solution. She asked if I had started the diet yet. I fudged and said I was just about to. She urged me not to wait and said that it was important that I follow it and restrict my calorie intake to 1,800 a day.

I thanked her for her help, but as I hung up the phone, I felt numb, lost, empty. I knew I had to get serious about this, but I felt like the little kid whose father gets transferred to another state and it's moving day and I'm about to leave all my old friends behind, the only friends I've ever had—burgers, French fries, chips, ice cream, pizza . . .

These were the friends who had stood by me through middle school, high school, and my first two years of college. But these were also the friends who had turned me into a 400-pounder. Most kids go away to college and gain the Freshman 15. In my case it was the Freshman 100.

I had looked forward to going away to college. When I started my freshman year at Indiana University, I was flush with a giddy sense of freedom and independence. I could do whatever I wanted now, take courses that I chose, stay up late without my parents nagging me to get to bed. I could do my homework or not do my homework; it was up to me. I was totally responsible for myself.

But there was one freedom that wasn't so good for me,

the freedom to pig out. I had an open meal plan, which meant that after I showed my meal card and entered the cafeteria, I could stay as long as I wanted and eat as much as I wanted, which is exactly what I did.

Remember, I loved food and I had a real soft spot for cafeteria fare. Most people turn up their noses at steam-table food, but not me.

Goulash, stuffed cabbage, ham steaks with pineapple slices, fried chicken, corn chowder, meatloaf, turkey with mashed potatoes and gravy—it was all good to me.

French toast, omelets, sausage patties, donuts, cheese Danish, Froot Loops, Lucky Charms—I couldn't wait to get up in the morning.

I'm ashamed to say that I actually told some of my dorm-mates that my goal for the year was to make the college food service lose money on me.

But I didn't confine myself to the cafeteria. We had a snack bar near my dorm that served food all day long and late into the night. Burgers, hot dogs, grilled cheese and bacon, onion rings, fries, frozen custard, cupcakes, ice cream sandwiches. Now this was freedom, I thought.

And then there was the take-out stuff that I could have delivered to the dorm, like subs and pizza and Chinese food. I got into the habit of ordering a large pizza and a bucket of soda every night as a midnight snack.

Later, when I figured it out, I realized was consuming about 10,000 calories a day. I was eating for five people . . . every day of the week.

When I was eating, I felt like a kid locked in the candy factory, but the rest of my college experience wasn't so rosy. For one thing my expanding girth had made me a prisoner inside my own body.

I couldn't go to restaurants unless they had seating that could accommodate me.

I couldn't get into the backseat of a car.

Forget about airplane seats.

Movie theaters and amusements parks—no way.

Dating? I wouldn't even consider it.

I became even more sedentary than I had been in high school. I was eating a lot more and doing a lot less—no wonder I was getting fatter. But denial is a funny thing—I knew what I was doing to myself, but at the same time I didn't want to know. I just wanted to go on the way I was and not worry about it. I was getting by, I told myself. Things weren't that bad.

But things *were* that bad, and there were reminders all around me. I just refused to recognize them. For one thing, I didn't pick my classes based on my intended major or any of my interests. I would examine the course catalog and make my selections based on the rooms where the classes were being held. Lecture halls were no good for me—the seats were too small. Any classroom that had those kinds of student desks that have the desktop attached to the seat were out, too. I looked for classes held in the seminar rooms that had long, open tables.

Then there was the matter of getting to class. Indiana University is a big school on a large campus. Class buildings are scattered pretty far apart, so they have a bus service for shuttling students around the campus. My dorm was just a five-minute walk from most of my classes—five minutes if you're not carrying 400-plus pounds. As I continued to overeat, it became harder and harder for me to walk even short distances. My knees ached. My back hurt. I was out of breath in no time and had to stop for frequent rests, bent over with my hands on my thighs, huffing and puffing. Eventually I got myself a bus pass and took the bus to my classes. But because of the circuitous bus route, I had to take a forty-five-minute trip around the campus to get to the buildings where my classes were. It was an incredible waste of time, but being in denial, I didn't let that bother me.

I didn't even let it bother me when I heard guys making cruel jokes about me. College guys living together are often crude. That's just the way it is. They usually don't mean to be hurtful, but they just can't help themselves. But as an overweight person, I had developed a knack for sensing a fat joke about to happen. For me, it's like reading the sky as a storm is brewing. Whenever I was with a group of rowdy guys, I could always feel it coming.

A bunch of guys would be out in the hallway at the dorm, just hanging out and horsing around. Then one of them would spot me. I could see from the keen look in his eye and his refusal to make eye contact with me that a fat joke was coming.

My method for dealing with this kind of situation was to head the joke off at the pass.

The joker would launch into his setup. "Jared's so fat, when he went to buy a water bed—"

"They threw a sheet over the ocean," I'd finish for him.

Everyone would laugh, me included, but I wasn't really

laughing. It was just my way of deflecting the blow. Jokes like these hurt, but not as much when I said the punch line.

I had other strategies for dealing with my big body. For one thing I never, ever took off my shirt in front of people. Way too embarrassing. I also bought clothes that were at least a size too big to camouflage my bulk. Loose clothes could cover up at least some of the harsh reality.

Buying clothes had always been a big source of embarrassment for me. By the time I was in fifth grade, I had graduated from regular to "husky" sizes. Now there's a euphemism all fat boys come to hate. Using the term "husky" is like saying an overweight woman is "full-figured." But I wasn't a husky for long. I remember shopping for school clothes with my mom just before I started seventh grade and finding out that I had outgrown the husky sizes. We had to walk to the other end of the mall, where the big and tall men's store was located. All the shirts we bought that day were adult 2XL—double extra large—and I was just eleven years old.

Of course, shopping in the big and tall shop did have one benefit. It had been almost impossible to find team jerseys and jackets in husky sizes, but there were usually plenty to choose from at the big and tall shop. The Indianapolis Colts were my favorite team, and I snapped up anything that displayed the Colts' horseshoe logo.

But becoming a human billboard—literally—for my favorite team was not a career option I was contemplating. At Indiana I was majoring in international business, but it occurred to me that my career goals might be derailed by my weight. I mean, here I was plotting and planning my daily routine around the size of the classrooms and how I could get there. I couldn't imagine any potential employer putting up with my unusual needs. Would an office reconfigure their cubicles so that I could have two or three? And I could never apply for jobs that involved air travel. I was an international business major who couldn't go international. I wasn't just fat anymore; I was obese. It was finally dawning on me that I actually had a disability.

When you think about it, people with serious problems, no matter what they are, all have a few things in common.

First, *the person affected is being held hostage by the problem.* What started out as a small issue—an interest in on-line sports betting, say—can quickly turn into something far greater. The problem just starts to grow and grow, like a tumor, and eventually you feel that it controls your life. Harmless gambling for points becomes gambling for dollars, seeking out bookies, betting lots of money, losing lots of money, borrowing more money to keep playing, telling yourself that all you want to do is "break even," when in fact you're hooked and you can't stop.

You begin to feel *trapped by the problem.* It can pin you into a corner. You know you have a problem, and you know you're in a bad situation, but at the same time you feel that there's nothing you can do about it. As I gained more and more weight, I felt more and more trapped because I knew it would take more and more work to take the weight off. I felt as if I were at the bottom of a pit with no way out.

When you feel trapped by a problem, you also tend to

feel isolated, as if *you're in a world that only you inhabit.*
You start to feel that no one else has ever had a problem
like yours, you're the only one. As I was growing up,
steadily gaining weight year by year, I created a world of
isolation. In one way it shielded me from hurt, but in truth
feeling alone hurt even more.

Finally, problems are embarrassing for the person who
has them, and *people naturally try to hide their problems.*
We've all heard stories about the "functional alcoholic"
who holds down a job, maintains a family life, and drinks
like a fish behind closed doors. Likewise, not all drug addicts are nodding off on the street. Some manage to walk a
precarious tightrope, maintaining a seemingly normal life
while addicted to marijuana, cocaine, speed, heroin, whatever. People with spending addictions learn how to inter-
cept credit card bills before anyone else sees them. Even
though I was a huge person who literally wore his problem
for the world to see, I also played the hiding game. As I
said, I never took my shirt off unless I was alone. I never
went to the beach. I used oversized clothes to cover up my
bulk. As ridiculous as it sounds, I did anything I could to
mask the fact that I weighed 425 pounds.

When the reality of my situation finally sunk in, I became determined to buckle down and get serious. I read the
diet booklet the endocrinologist had given me cover to
cover, read it again, really studied it. The diet called for
1,800 calories a day maximum, which was about 16 percent of what I usually ate. But that didn't bother me. It actually motivated me. I started making lists of the good
foods I would buy. I asked my mom to show me how to

cook them. I had moved off campus after my second year at IU, and I imagined the kitchen at my apartment, visualizing myself cooking healthy food there, then eating it at the kitchen table. I was psyched.

I planned to start the diet once I got back to Bloomington, where IU is located. I didn't want my family or anyone else watching me and monitoring my progress. Even the thought of joining a support group made me cringe. Losing weight was a personal thing, and I had to do it by myself. No cheerleaders, no critics, no spying eyes.

The only person I would share this with was JL, my old friend from high school who had been my roommate in the dorm. We now shared the apartment off campus, so it would have been hard to hide my new diet from him. But I was okay with that. JL was cool. I trusted him. When we'd both gotten into Indiana, we'd decided to room together rather than risk living with strangers who might not be as understanding of our situations.

JL was a serious student majoring in biochemistry and premed. He was also a physical fitness fanatic who spent at least an hour a day working out at the gym. This passion of his never came between us until we started living together.

"Jared," he said one morning as I was slathering peanut butter on a slice of toast, "why don't you come down to the gym with me this morning?"

I just stared at him. He was suited up in his sweats and running shoes. This wasn't the first time he'd invited me.

"No thanks," I said, then took a big bite out of my toast.

"But, Jared, you might like it," he said. "And it would help you."

I gave him a dirty look. I didn't want to go anywhere near a gym. I didn't even like talking about it. And to work out with someone as fit as JL would have been humiliating.

"Hey, I'm worried about you, man," JL said in his typically blunt way. "You should lose some weight."

"We've had this conversation before, JL. I told you, I don't like gyms." I continued to eat my breakfast, hoping he'd just go away.

"Why?" he said. "Why don't you like gyms?"

"Because I don't, okay? Now don't ask me again."

The truth was that I didn't like being seen, and to me that's what gyms were all about—skinny people checking each other out to see who was skinny and who wasn't. If I went to a place like that, I knew everyone would be staring at me.

But JL was persistent. I knew he intended to pester me until I gave in. "Listen to me, Jared—" he started.

"No, you listen to me," I shouted over him. "I've told you a million times: I don't like gyms."

"But, Jared—"

"And if you keep bugging me about it, maybe we shouldn't live together anymore."

A tense, awkward silence filled the room. "You don't have to do that," he finally said. "I don't want to live with anybody else."

"Okay then."

"Jared, I'm just concerned about you. That's all."

"I . . . I appreciate that you're concerned, but . . ." I was so angry I could barely talk. But I valued him as a friend, and I didn't want to lose him. Even though I'd thought about living by myself at one point, I was never really serious about it. JL was my best friend then, and he still is today. That's why I wasn't worried about JL knowing about my new diet. I knew he'd approve, and he knew that I wouldn't want to talk about it. He'd respect that.

The first thing I'd done after returning to school and dropping off my bags at the apartment was get back in the car and drive down to the grocery store. With the diet booklet in my hand, I found a cart near the entrance and headed inside. I was a man on a mission.

I attacked the produce section first, a part of the store I'd rarely visited. I filled a plastic bag with ears of corn. I got lettuce and cucumbers for salad and a bag of peeled baby carrots.

I moved on to the aisles, scouring the shelves for the words "fat free." I found fat-free salad dressing and picked out two different kinds. I tossed in a big plastic squeeze bottle of mustard. No more fatty mayonnaise for me.

I went to the meat cases and loaded up on poultry. Good-bye greasy burgers and the sausage and pepperoni I used to order on my pizzas. It was going to be turkey and chicken from now on.

I sailed down the snack aisle—dangerous terrain for me—but I looked past my beloved Doritos and Ruffles and scooped up some bags of low-fat pretzels and moved on.

I kept going, like an explorer discovering uncharted territories. I checked out the stats on the fat-free pudding containers and compared them to the guidelines in the booklet. They were okay so I put a six-pack of vanilla and a six-pack of chocolate in the cart.

I tossed whole-grain breakfast cereals into my basket. Bacon and eggs and pancakes dripping with butter and syrup were now a thing of the past, I said to myself. I was determined not to miss them.

I stocked up on packages of frozen vegetables—green beans, broccoli, peas, corn—so that I wouldn't have to worry about things going bad in the refrigerator.

I found room in my cart for a gallon of orange juice, a gallon of apple juice, a gallon of skim milk, and a loaf of bread. The cart was pretty full, and I figured that much food would keep me for at least a week, so I moved on to the checkout line. I was already feeling better as I unloaded my food onto the conveyor belt. My new diet was off to a good start, I thought.

When I got home, my next project was finding places to put the food in our tiny apartment. Neither JL nor I was very domestic. He was a little better, but neither of us usually kept much food in the house. In my case it was mainly junk food—chips and nuts, stuff like that. But now that I'd discovered a whole new world of healthy eating, I had to get organized and store my provisions. I was amazed to discover that there really was an important use for kitchen cabinets. (My jumbo bags of chips—if they stayed around that long—lived on the kitchen table or on top of the refrigerator.) So now I took over one entire cabinet for myself and filled it to the gills.

I moved on to the fridge, putting all of JL's stuff on one shelf while I filled up the rest of the shelves with my newly acquired food. I stocked the freezer with all the great new veggies I was going to eat. By the time I was through, I was exhausted. And I still had to cook the food! I was building up an appetite just getting ready to eat healthy.

I decided to take a break. I sat down in my favorite chair and played video games for a while, usually a dangerous situation for me with regard to food. Playing Nintendo and snacking went together like . . . well, bread and butter, bacon and eggs, burgers and fries. But I was determined and I fought off the impulse. I was going to wait and make myself a good dinner at dinnertime, not before. No more eating in between meals. That was part of the diet.

My stomach rumbled, begging for a little something to tide me over, but I was resolute. I held out until five thirty. I figured that was probably a good time to start cooking since I had only a vague idea of how long it would take to cook a meal from scratch. My first problem was finding the pots and pans. I knew we had them, but since JL and I never cooked, I was clueless as to where they'd be. I looked through the cabinets over the counter and in the oven, hoping they'd be where I could easily reach them. Unfortunately, I realized, they were probably where I didn't want them to be, in the cabinets under the counter. I was forced to get down on my already aching knees.

I opened the first cabinet and found nothing but garbage bags and a box of aluminum foil. I took out the foil and tossed it up on the counter. I'd probably need that later for leftovers, I thought.

In the next cabinet I found the pots and pans huddling way in the back as if they were trying to hide from me. This was annoying. For a normal-sized person, reaching back there would be nothing, but for me it was an exercise in precision balancing, pain endurance, and strength as I held myself up on one arm as I reached inside. I considered getting the broom to scoop the pots and pans toward the front of the cabinet, but that would involve getting up and getting back down on the floor again, and that was just too daunting to even think about. After several tries, I managed to bat a couple of pots and a broiling pan toward the front of the cabinet like a hungry bear knocking down a beehive for the honey.

Getting back on my feet was excruciating. I had to pull over a chair to haul myself up and lean on the counter to support myself until I was reasonably sure my sore knees would hold me. My face was flushed and my shirt was drenched with sweat, and I knew that turning on the oven would make me even more uncomfortable. Still, I was motivated and looking forward to my first healthy meal.

I set down the diet booklet on the counter and got to work. I'd decided to cook a chicken dinner—a broiled skinless chicken breast, a portion of green beans, a slice of plain white bread, and a small container of fat-free pudding for dessert. I rinsed off the chicken breast and seasoned it, then put it under the broiler in the oven. The diet plan called for green beans to go with the chicken, so I took out a package of frozen green beans. It was frozen solid in a block, so I threw the whole thing in a pot with a little water and turned on a flame under it. I'd eat the rest tomorrow as leftovers, I told myself.

Fifteen minutes later the chicken was cooked, and the

greens beans were hot. I arranged my meal on a plate and took it to the table. I was dead tired but eager to taste the fruits of my labor. I cut into the chicken and took a bite.

Not bad, I thought. I was kind of shocked but also pleased. This just might work.

I dug in and cleaned my plate, eating everything I was allotted. When I was finished, I was overjoyed. I'd actually prepared a healthy dinner and eaten it. I felt as if I'd discovered America!

There was only one problem. It wasn't very much food.

My usual dinners consisted of a double half-pound burger with extra cheese and bacon, an extra-large order of fries, and a bucket of regular, not diet, soda. Five minutes after finishing my healthy dinner, I was starving. I looked over at the pot of green beans on the stove. I'd made the entire package, but the booklet said I was supposed to eat only a third of it in one meal. I glanced at the loaf of bread on the counter. I could have easily scarfed down half of it, but I'd already had my allotted single slice. I heaved a heavy sigh. This wasn't going to be easy. Fortunately I was so tired from shopping and cooking, I passed out on the couch before nine o'clock and that kept me from cheating on my diet.

The next morning I consulted the booklet before attempting breakfast. It recommended a small glass of orange juice and a bowl of whole-wheat flakes with skim milk. Black coffee or plain tea optional. Okay, that was easy enough. Well, easy but *not* enough.

My stomach moaned and groaned the whole morning. For lunch I had a big salad with diet dressing at the campus cafeteria, washing it down with a big glass of water. I was eating like a big bunny.

Dinner rolled around, and once again I had to do the cooking. Another chicken breast, an ear of corn (no butter), a slice of bread, and another cup of pudding. This meal took a little longer to cook because of the corn, and that made me grouchy. Actually the whole diet was making me grouchy. I was starving. My body cried out for more calories. But as miserable as I was, I wasn't going to give in to my cravings. I was determined to succeed.

Fortunately—I guess—I was once again exhausted after dinner, and I soon conked out on the couch, which prevented me from eating any more. But I didn't sleep well. My rumbling stomach kept waking me up. The next morning I faced the same tiny breakfast as the day before—cereal and juice—and now I was grouchier than ever. By the end of the day the prospect of another chicken breast with a portion of the leftover green beans from the first night turned me into an ogre. I was Shrek before he got nice.

I stuck it out for two more days, desperate to make this diet work. But I was so tired by the end of the day, I couldn't get my homework done. And my stomach made so much noise I didn't want to go out. People might think I'd swallowed a midget whole, and he was yelling for help inside my gut.

I remember sitting at the kitchen table on the morning of the fifth day, staring at a little bowl of the same bland cereal I'd been eating all week. I just couldn't face it. I couldn't do it anymore. This diet wasn't for me.

JL was just coming out of his room to go to class.

"Hey, JL," I said, "if you want anything in the fridge, just take it. The stuff in the cabinets, too."

"Oh," JL said. "Okay. . . . Thanks."

He knew this meant I was throwing in the towel, but he was sensitive enough to my situation not to say anything.

"I'll see you later," he said as he slung his backpack over his shoulder and went out the door.

As soon as the door closed, I hauled myself out of the chair and picked up the booklet from the counter. I stepped on the pedal of the trash can and dropped it in. The lid closed, and I felt like a terrible failure.

Now I know what you're thinking: "Jared, you blew it! You failed. What's the lesson here?"

Well, it's true, I did fail at my first attempt at dieting, but the important thing is that I *tried*. I wasn't in denial about my weight anymore, and I wasn't just thinking about it. I was actually *doing* something.

Do Something

- When trying to deal with your problem, don't limit yourself to one approach. Try lots of different things.
- As you search for a solution, stay open-minded. Consider everything.
- Don't play the "numbers game," spinning the facts to make them seem better than they really are. If you weigh 400 pounds, you weigh 400 pounds. Drinking a six-pack of beer every night of the week is not healthy even if you say you're not get-

ting fall-down drunk. Making excuses won't help you out of your rut.

- People with serious problems often go to great lengths to hide their true condition. Instead, channel all that time and energy toward solving the problem.

LESSON 3

Reach for the Stars

Whatever your problem is, it's a really big thing to you. So why would you tackle it in a small way? Setting a series of baby-step goals might be a way of creating attainable stepping stones for some people, but for most of us it simply minimizes a serious problem. If you tell yourself that you're going to lose 10 pounds, then 10 pounds more, then 10 pounds more, and what you really need to lose is in the triple digits, you're just setting yourself up for drudgery and frustration, and that just leads to failure and a trip down to Mickey D's.

If your life were a movie, you'd be the hero, right? It would be an epic struggle for survival and happiness. It would have many sequels, like *Star Wars*.

Okay, let's stay with the *Star Wars* analogy for a minute. You, being the hero, can't overcome the Dark Side by taking out one clone trooper here and another clone trooper there. A real hero has to confront the big problem head-on, fly right into the Death Star and blow it to smithereens. Your goal has to be as important as you are, and since you're the hero of your own life, you should set a goal that's worthy of you.

Small goals are easily forgotten, swept under the rug, put off until tomorrow.

Big goals can't be ignored. They become a quest rather than just an annoying addition to your daily routine. A big goal involves struggle and sacrifice, and you must convince yourself that you're up to the task. On the other hand, if you fail to achieve a small goal, so what? It's no big deal. It's just a little setback. But with a greater goal, something important is at stake. In my case it was my future. Losing weight was literally a life-or-death matter for me because if I didn't drop a couple hundred pounds, I was going to die.

Once I started to see my problem in these terms, I became much more focused. I realized that I needed a diet plan that would work for me, but I also realized that I couldn't depend on the diet to do the work for me.

A lot of overweight people drink diet sodas and use artificial sweeteners in their coffee all the time and they never seem to lose weight. Why? Because they're hoping the product will do the work for them. This is the same as a couch potato saying he's going to run a marathon, so he goes out and buys the most expensive pair of running shoes on the market. Obviously the shoes alone won't do it for him. He has to get up off the couch, train hard, get sweaty, get dirty, endure the pain. That's how you finish a marathon.

It's the same with losing weight. Or quitting cigarettes. Or getting off drugs or booze. Or facing your family problems. You can't win the struggle without struggling. You can't be passive and think that Diet Coke or methadone or nicotine chewing gum will do it for you. *You* have to do it for you.

You can't be a minor character in the movie of your own life. You have to be the hero and act heroically. Confront the monster head-on. Reach for the stars!

After I gave up on my first diet, I felt that I had failed big-time. All the healthy food that I had bought and given to JL was still in the cabinets and refrigerator, reminding me that I'd failed. Every pizza, every burger, every taco, every burrito, every liter of soda, every single French fry that I ate after that reminded me that I'd failed. I felt bad, but unlike other times in my overweight life, this time I didn't get depressed. I still wanted to lose weight, and I hadn't given up hope. That burning ember was still inside of me, like the last glowing charcoal in the barbecue at the end of a summer's day. A raging fire of success could still be ignited from that ember. I truly believed that.

Most people with serious problems have what I call "lottery-ticket dreams." *Someday I'll be rich,* they think, but they have no plan for making more money. Every day they have all the hope in the world that luck will shine down on them. But as everyone knows—them included—the chances of hitting the lottery are incredibly small. Still, every day these people line up to buy more and more lottery tickets.

Obese people, drug addicts, smokers, gamblers, alco-

holics, spend-a-holics all look to the horizon for the day
when they will be free of their addictions. The problem is
they don't know how to get to that day. In most cases they
don't even know how to *dream* about getting there. It's just
a hazily envisioned change that will happen sometime in
the nebulous future. That was exactly how I was. I saw myself losing a lot of weight someday and getting down to a
manageable size, but I didn't have a clue as to how I was
going to get there.

Now, I know what you're thinking. "Why didn't you
just go on another diet, Jared? There are dozens of diet
books in the bookstore. Why didn't you just pick one up
and follow it?"

Well, I did that. And I'll be the first to say that experts
and programs can be a great help when trying to overcome
a huge problem, *but not for everyone.* Diet books and diet
programs can also be crutches that keep you disabled as
you run from one to another, searching for a solution. That
certainly was the case with me. I kept looking to outside
sources for a miracle, like the guy who keeps going back to
the convenience store for more lottery tickets. Hitting the
lottery involves blind luck—you just stand there and it happens or it doesn't. Actively changing your life means taking
a step, then another step, then another toward your goal.

The 1,800-calories-a-day diet was a bust, but I was sure
there was another diet out there that would work. It was
just a matter of finding it. That's why there are so many
bestselling diet books and diet products on the market.
People are always looking for something that will work for
them, and I fit right into that category.

I felt that a big problem with the healthy food diet was the amount of time I had to put into it. Perhaps if I didn't have to spend so much time preparing the food, maybe I'd have an easier time sticking with a diet. That's when a new solution hit me: frozen foods. I'd heard all about the various frozen entrées created for dieters, and I'd seen the ads on TV that featured people who had experienced dramatic weight loss. I never paid much attention to before-and-after pictures—that was them, not me, I thought—but when I started seeing photos of people as bad off and in some case worse off than I was, I started to consider diet frozen foods. If it worked for those people, why shouldn't it work for me?

I gathered my courage and went back to the grocery store, steering my cart straight to the frozen-food aisle. I scanned the shelves behind the frosty glass of refrigerator cases until I found the low-fat entrées. As soon as I saw the colorful pictures of hot meals on the boxes, I knew that this was going to be a lot more fun than the last time. Those scrumptious photos stared back at me, like puppies in the pet-store window, begging me to take them home. There were chicken dinners with creamy sauces, chicken enchiladas, chili, spaghetti and meatballs, lasagna, fettuccine Alfredo, pot roast, meatloaf, Salisbury steak, and, wonder of all wonders, pizza! Several kinds of pizza! I got a little light-headed with joy. If I could eat pizza and lose weight, that would be like . . . like eating pizza!

I loaded up my cart with entrées from all the companies that made diet food and pushed on to the checkout, gleefully stacking frozen-food boxes on the conveyor belt for the clerk to ring me up. I'd bought so much food, when I got home, I had to take out the ice trays to fit it all in the freezer.

I was delirious as I packed my new purchases into the freezer. Not only were they low-calorie, in most cases these boxes contained complete meals with the side dish included, just like the old-fashioned TV dinners. I didn't have to worry about making different things in different pots and pans and timing it so that they were all ready at the same time. All I had to do was stick one of these babies in the microwave, zap it for three minutes, and *shazam!* it would be ready. It couldn't have been more convenient, I thought. I couldn't wait to have my first one, and I already knew which one it would be.

At dinnertime I pulled out my first meal—lasagna with meat sauce—and stuck it in the microwave. I watched it through the glass window as it turned round and round. The bell dinged, and I pulled it out, immediately peeling off the plastic top. It smelled absolutely delicious. A very good sign, I thought. I grabbed a fork from the drawer and carried my meal to the table.

I dug in, spearing a forkful and blowing on it to cool it. The aroma was amazing. This was going to be great, I thought.

Then I tasted it.

I can't tell you how awful and disappointing it was.

I tried a second bite, hoping that the first one was a fluke, but I was frowning as I chewed. I went to the garbage can to fish out the box it came in to make sure this was what I thought it was. Maybe it was yak parmesan and

I'd assumed from the picture that it was lasagna. But, no, I was right. This was supposed to be lasagna with meat sauce, but it didn't even come close. The taste was weird, and the consistency was chalky. I mean, it looked perfect. The cheese stretched the way it was supposed to, and the sauce looked right, but it was inedible. I know it's a cliché, but in this case the box probably did taste better than what was inside.

But I wasn't about to give up on these meals yet. I forced the lasagna down and told myself that this probably wasn't that company's best dish and I just wouldn't buy it again. The others would be better, I told myself. Especially the pizza.

But I was so wrong, it broke my heart. The pizza I had for lunch the next day was a pitiful imitation of a real pizza. The cheese tasted like melted plastic. The sauce was no better than uncooked tomato paste. The crust was like soggy cardboard. I seriously wondered if this was the company's cruel response to the box-being-better-than-the-food cliché.

For my next meal, I heated up the turkey dinner. Once again it smelled pretty good, and it triggered memories of delicious Thanksgiving dinners I'd had at home. But the taste was a huge letdown. The meat was dry, and the mashed potatoes and stuffing were blander than bland. And with this one, I discovered that these dinners didn't always heat up evenly. One bite would be hot enough to burn the skin off the roof of my mouth while the next was as cold as ice. Well, that's no problem, I thought. Another minute in the microwave warmed up the potatoes and stuffing nicely, but the turkey turned to shoe leather and the gravy burned to a dark sticky solid.

Still, I was willing to give these dinners a chance. There were a lot of others in the freezer, many to choose from. I figured there had to be some good ones. I just happened to pick the bad ones first.

But there weren't any good ones.

The meatloaf tasted like pressed sawdust.

I was convinced the Salisbury steak was made from old ground-up car tires.

The fettuccine noodles were gummy, and the Alfredo sauce looked and tasted like glue.

The spaghetti and meatballs? Forget about it. String and mothballs.

I wanted to like these meals, I really did, but the next time I went to the freezer to pick one out, I hesitated, remembering all the bad tastes I'd experienced. I stuck out my foot and looked down at my sneaker, thinking it probably tasted better than any of these frozen meals. That's when I gave up on the frozen food diet.

I walked over to JL's room. He was bent over his desk, studying. "JL," I said, "if you want any of those frozen dinners I bought, help yourself—"

He held up his open hand and showed me his palm. He wrinkled his nose and made a stinky face as he shook his head.

I went back to the kitchen and emptied out the freezer, dropping one box after another into the trash. I was doubly frustrated. I'd spent a lot of money on these foods, and now they were going to waste. But even though I was giving up on this approach, I wasn't giving up on the idea of slimming down.

Late one night about a week later a new solution came to me as I was watching television. A commercial came on for diet shakes. According to the announcer, the tried-and-true formula for weight loss was "one delicious shake for breakfast, another delicious shake for lunch, and a sensible dinner of your choice." The commercial showed the usual before-and-after pictures—dumpy housewives turned into drop-dead gorgeous babes, flabby used-car salesmen with bad comb-overs transformed into gleaming-toothed body builders—but that wasn't what impressed me. It was the "sensible dinner" part. The shakes sounded pretty tasty, and they came in several flavors including vanilla, chocolate, strawberry, and coffee. I couldn't imagine that they could taste any worse than those chemical-flavored frozen dinners. But getting to pick my own dinner was extremely appealing to me. If I could tough out the two liquid meals, then I'd be able to have a regular, solid dinner. Just as long as it was "sensible."

Well, the shake company had a different definition for "delicious" than I did. Their product tasted horrible and totally artificial. But I was willing to put up with the taste if it worked.

Unfortunately I also had a problem with the shake company's definition of "sensible dinner." Their notion of a sensible dinner was more in line with my first diet, the 1,800-calories-a-day diet—a skinless chicken breast, a half cup of string beans, one slice of bread, and a dollop of low-cal pudding. My definition was a bit different.

After drinking a terrible 16-ounce shake for breakfast and a second terrible 16-ounce shake for lunch, by the time dinner rolled around I was ravenous. The first couple of days on the shake diet, I tried to put together dinners from whatever we had in the house—tuna salad, macaroni and cheese, canned beef stew—but that wasn't very much food for me, and I wasn't satisfied.

By the third day, I was like a hungry T. rex on the hunt. I had dutifully drunk my two shakes for breakfast and lunch, but when it was time for dinner, the cupboards were pretty bare so I decided to go out to the local Chinese restaurant that had an all-you-can-eat buffet for $8.99. I figured I deserved a treat for all my good efforts.

Now, I knew this was going to be bad for me, but whenever I really wanted to eat something, I could twist logic until the choice made perfect sense. Chicken was on all the diets I'd tried so far, so I figured I'd just eat whatever chicken they had at the buffet. Including deep-fried General Tso's chicken in that yummy sweet sauce.

The buffet also had pepper steak, lo mein, mu shu pork, fried rice, egg rolls, pot stickers, and about a dozen other dishes, all of them there for the taking. I swore to myself that I would stick to the diet and eat "sensibly," that I wouldn't pig out, but I was so hungry and the buffet table was too tempting. I just couldn't help myself. I loaded up my plate, cleaned it in no time, then loaded it up again. I went back for thirds, then finally finished off the meal with a few more egg rolls and a fistful of fortune cookies. The owner of the restaurant scowled at me as I went to the cash register to pay my bill. He'd definitely lost money that night, and I felt terrible for falling off the wagon again. But, hey, who was I kidding? Any diet that left me this hungry by the end of the day wasn't going to work for me. As soon as I got home, I tossed my four canisters of powdered shake mix into the garbage.

I went to bed that night frustrated and disappointed with myself. I'd failed again, and as a result I didn't like myself very much. I felt that deep down no one in the world knew what I was going through, not even JL. My self-esteem was just about nonexistent. I tossed and turned all night, worrying myself sick. By dawn my stomach was rumbling again, and I just wanted to tell it to shut the hell up. I'd reached my lowest point yet. I felt as if I were stuck at the bottom of a pit, and I didn't see any way of getting out. As I wallowed in self-pity, I fast-forwarded my life, imagining myself gaining more weight, and my life becoming more and more restricted. I wouldn't be able to finish college. I'd never find a decent job. I'd have to move back in with my parents, permanently. No insurance company would ever cover me, and I'd probably end up dying young.

But as dejected as I was, there was still a faint voice deep within me that refused to be silenced. "Don't give up, Jared," the voice said. "Keep going. You'll find a solution."

I still had hope.

But what exactly was I hoping for?

As the sun started to come up, I stared at the ceiling and tried to analyze my situation objectively. I had to lose weight—that was obvious. But how much weight? What was my goal? The diet books I'd read all said the same thing—start with a manageable goal, 5 pounds, 10 pounds, something you can achieve pretty easily, so that you'll be inspired to lose more. But come on, I was 425 pounds. What was losing 10 pounds going to do for me? If you take a wheelbarrow full of dirt off a mountain, you've still got a mountain, right? I knew that conventional diet wisdom wasn't going to work for me. I needed a better goal, a worthy goal, something I could reach for, even if it seemed like I was reaching for the stars. I needed to figure out what I really wanted.

In my insomniac ruminations, I went over it again and again in my head until I realized what I really wanted. *I wanted to be happy. I wanted to be happy with my body.* What I really wanted was to be able to step on a scale and see my weight under 200. It was a fantasy I'd carried with me for years, like a favorite scene in a cherished old movie. I knew that this was a nearly impossible goal, but that's what I truly wanted: not to be embarrassed getting on a scale. To feel *good* about myself getting on a scale. To see concrete proof that I was a normal-sized person.

As I started to drift off to sleep around 6:00 A.M., I knew I had come to a major revelation. I finally knew what I really wanted. I wanted to drop at least 226 pounds so that I could get on a scale and see 199.

I just had to figure out how to do it.

Reach for the Stars

- If you want to achieve big results, set a big goal for yourself. If you want to lose 100 pounds, don't tell yourself that you'll do it in 10-pound increments.

Small goals are easily forgotten, but big goals can't be ignored. Shoot for the moon and tell yourself you're going to lose 100 pounds.

- You can't win a struggle without struggling. You have to do the "heavy lifting" yourself.
- You are the hero of our own life, so act like a hero. Confront your problem head-on.
- Get rid of your "lottery-ticket dreams." *(Someday I'll be rich. . . . Someday I'll be thin. . . . Someday I'll be sober. . . .)* Wishing and hoping won't make it happen. Stop dreaming and start doing.

LESSON 4

Find Your Personal Spark

After three failed attempts at dieting, I came to realize that I needed something to spur me on when I felt my resolve weakening. We all seem to keep a squirming bag of amorphous fears and dreads hidden in the attics of our lives. We try to hide them and forget about them, but I decided to bring mine out into the open and use them to my advantage. I called them my personal sparks. They were very powerful incentives because they were unique to me, mine and mine alone, and therefore I couldn't ignore them.

Cultivate your own personal sparks and draw upon them whenever you're in danger of veering off the path to your goal.

Pull one of the little demons out of your secret bag and examine it closely. What is it? A fear. And a fear is a negative.

Now turn it around to make it a positive, an incentive to avoid being harmed by that fear.

If you're a shopoholic, what's your worst fear? Maxing out your credit cards and getting repeated calls from the credit card companies demanding payment? Well, make that your personal spark. Think about having to deal with a nasty collection agency or a corporate legal department every time you're tempted to buy something you know you really shouldn't.

Addicted to marijuana? Imagine what it would be like to get arrested for possession of an illegal substance. Think of the legal hassles and the personal embarrassment. Imagine losing your job because of it. Think of all these things before you roll yourself a joint or buy yourself a new supply.

Do you have anger issues and take it out on your wife and kids? Next time you're ready to explode, imagine them leaving you. Imagine your wife filing for divorce. Imagine your kids never speaking to you again. It might help you keep your temper in check before you explode.

Keep your personal sparks in the back of your mind and use them whenever you need them, the way a cardiac patient might carry nitroglycerin pills, just in case. Hopefully you'll never need them, but if you do, don't hesitate to use them.

There were a couple of things that had happened to me before I started dieting that took on greater significance when I got serious about losing weight. They were fears that had been dwelling in my mind and nibbling away at my self-confidence for some time. One of these fears related to a terrible incident that had come without warning, hitting me like a meteor falling out of the sky. It was so bad I had nightmares about it for a long time, and even now I cringe just thinking about it.

As I continued to gain weight in high school, my sleeping habits changed. I found myself sleeping more and more at night and nodding off during the day, too. By the time I entered college, I would go to bed for the night, sleep twelve hours straight through, then wake up and fall back to sleep without even realizing it. I would suddenly just doze off, usually during class. Of course, being in denial about my situation, I didn't let my weird sleeping patterns concern me, though in hindsight I should have been *very* concerned. Sleeping that much isn't normal.

I also snored, and I was told that it wasn't a gentle Rip-van-Winkle-snoozing-under-a-tree kind of snore. My snore was equivalent to gale-force winds. I snored so badly I could have been the subject of a special report on the Weather Channel.

My roommate, JL, never complained about my snoring, so I didn't realize how bad it was until I left our suite at the dorm one morning and noticed that someone had put a new message on our floor's message board. It was a white plastic board, the kind that's used with washable ink markers. The message was impossible to ignore. It had been written in big block letters in thick red ink: WHY DON'T YOU SNORE OUT YOUR BUTT SOME MORE, JARED!!!

The author's anger was in his boldfaced penmanship as well as his words. I must have kept him up with my snoring the night before, but I couldn't believe that the sound could carry from my room inside my suite, out into the hallway, and into his room in his suite.

Whoever this guy was, he was just being a jerk, I thought. It wasn't me who kept him up, I told myself. Couldn't be. No one snores that loudly.

But that's how denial works. The evidence of my problem was all around me, sometimes screaming at me, but I simply refused to acknowledge it.

Until the end of my second year of college.

Classes had ended, and I had taken the last of my exams. The university didn't let students store their belongings in the dorms over the summer, so I had to haul my stuff home by the end of May. I had a lot to move—a minifridge, a TV set, a boom box, a desktop computer, boxes of books, CDs, DVDs, clothes, shoes, the usual college-kid stuff. It was more than I could fit into my car in one trip, so I asked my parents if I could borrow their minivan. They said, sure, no problem. Indiana University was just an hour away from my parents' house. I could easily drive home, pick up the van, load it up, and drive back in one day. No problem, I thought.

It was around eleven in the morning by the time I left the campus. School was over, so I'd slept late and then had a leisurely breakfast. I drove my gold Toyota Corolla—

(Yes, I know what you're thinking. *Jared, you fit into a compact car?* Well, yes, I did. It was a tight fit, and not nearly as comfortable as my previous car, my beloved red 1993 Honda Civic. I loved that car, but more on that later.)

As I was saying, I drove the Corolla home, stayed long

enough to have lunch with my mom, then drove the mini-van back to school.

It was the middle of the afternoon by the time I pulled up to Read Hall, a relatively modern six-story dorm. In the lobby I snatched one of the big laundry carts that the university provided for students to move in and out with, pushed it onto an elevator, and squeezed in with it, taking it up to the sixth floor, where my suite was located. Ironically the heaviest student at IU lived on the top floor of one of the highest buildings on campus.

I filled the cart to the gills with books and clothes and brought it out to the van. My shirt was drenched with sweat as I unloaded the cart.

I went back up and put my mini-fridge and two boxes of videotapes and CDs into the cart. I took them down and slid them into the back of the van. The fridge wasn't that heavy, but it was awkward for me to move and took more effort than I'd thought it would.

I stopped off at the vending-machine room on the first floor of the dorm for a soda and a bag of chips before I finished up. I'd left my computer and television set for last, not wanting to leave them alone in the van.

The computer monitor was heavy and cumbersome, and my back ached as I lowered it into the deep cart. Same thing with the TV set. The weight was lopsided, and I had to be careful not to drop it. By the time I wedged the computer into the cart and put the keyboard on top, I was pooped. I sat down on the bed and rested for a while. I thought about going down to the van for a dry shirt, but I didn't want to waste any more time than I had to. If I left

soon, I wouldn't get caught in rush-hour traffic around Indianapolis.

I hauled myself off the bed and pushed my last load
down to the van. Out in the parking lot my shoulders
popped and my back protested as I struggled to lift the
heavy items out of my cart, but eventually I did it. I walked
the empty cart back to the lobby, huffing and puffing, and
dropped off my key at the dorm office.

"Have a good summer," the girl collecting keys said to
me.

"Yeah . . . you too," I said. I was breathing so hard I
was barely able to get the words out.

She narrowed her eyes at me. "You okay?" she said.

"Yeah . . . I'm fine." I waved good-bye and trudged back
to the van. I really wanted to beat the traffic.

I climbed into the minivan, started the engine, and put
on the air-conditioning full blast. I sat there for a minute
and let the cold air hit my face. It felt so good I thought
about tipping the seat back and just resting for a while, but
it was getting late. I knew that if I got caught in rush hour,
my trip home would take twice as long.

I switched on the radio. The Dave Matthews Band was
playing "What Would You Say?" That perked me up, so I
turned up the volume.

I backed out of the parking space and headed for Route
37. Five minutes later I was whizzing down the road, heading for home. There was more traffic than when I'd started
out that morning, but it wasn't bad. A big rig came up fast
behind me and sat on my tail, the trucker obviously desperate to make time. My parents' minivan was no match

for a trailer truck, so I pulled into the far right lane and gave him the road. He immediately zoomed past me.

After a while I glanced at the clock in the dashboard radio. It was ten after four. I could still beat the rush hour if I stepped on it. I was a little tired, and I thought about pulling over to rest for a while, but I was almost halfway there. I could stick it out for another half hour, I told myself. I turned up the volume on the radio and adjusted the air vents so that the cold air was blowing right at me. I pulled into the middle lane and drove a little faster.

Another big rig came up fast behind me, flashing his lights and blowing his horn. He got within three feet of my rear bumper and stayed there. Not a very subtle hint. I immediately signaled and got out of his way before he rolled over me, the jerk.

A few minutes later I saw a sign for Indianapolis up ahead. Another fifteen minutes and I'll be home, I thought.

Bon Jovi was on the radio, "Living on a Prayer." I liked that song and started humming along with it. It made up for the nasty trucker who'd tailgated me. I really got into the song, nodding to the beat, singing along with the chorus.

And that is the last thing I remember.

When I woke up again, the minivan was rumbling and bouncing violently, making all kinds of awful noises. I gripped the wheel for dear life. There was no road ahead of me, just grass. I looked right and left and realized I was on the grassy area on the side of the highway. But I was traveling at highway speed! I slammed on the brakes. The van swerved. Instantly I took my foot off the brake pedal and steered into the swerve as if I were on ice. The van straightened out, and I pumped the brake steadily until I could bring it to a halt.

My heart was pounding like a jackhammer in my chest. How did I get here? I wondered. What the hell happened?

I looked in the rearview mirror. Tire tracks scarred the ground behind me.

In the back of the van all my stuff had shifted to one side.

I was sweating buckets despite the air-conditioning. I couldn't figure out how I'd gotten there.

The radio was still on, Bon Jovi still blasting "Living on a Prayer."

I turned it off, dazed and confused. I must have just blacked out for no reason, I thought. I rubbed my face and shook the cobwebs out of my head.

Then I started to put it all together. Falling asleep without warning was a symptom of sleep apnea. It happened to me all the time. I could remember a few occasions when I'd been drowsy behind the wheel, but I'd never actually fallen asleep while driving. Not until now.

I must have suddenly dozed off, and the van drifted off the road and into the grass. The noise and the jostling must have woken me up. I figured it must have happened in a matter of seconds because the song was still playing. Thank God the grassy area was flat. I could've been killed.

My heart started pounding harder as that thought sunk in. Not only could I have killed myself, I could have killed other people, too. I thought about school buses and vans full of kids and overturned trailer trucks and massive pileups.

My weight problem had struck again. I couldn't even

rely on my own body to do something as simple as drive anymore. I was a danger to myself and everyone around me. I worried that I'd never be able to drive again. The bigger I got the smaller my world was becoming. If I couldn't drive, I wouldn't be able to get around. My activities were already severely limited by my weight. If I lost my driver's license, people in wheelchairs would have more options than I would.

My mind went into a tailspin as I imagined all kinds of terrible worst-case scenarios. I'm not sure how long it took me to get myself together and get back on the road, but I didn't beat the rush-hour traffic that afternoon, and I was glad that I didn't. I was terrified that I would suddenly fall asleep again, but at least I wouldn't cause much damage crawling along in bumper-to-bumper traffic.

It was 6:30 P.M. by the time I pulled into the driveway at my parents' house. As I walked in the front door, I immediately smelled dinner. My parents, my brother, and my sister were at the dining room table, just getting started.

"Jared," my mother said, "where've you been? We've been waiting for you."

"Stop for a snack?" my brother, Adam, asked in his typically snarky way.

My sister, Jessica, threw him a dirty look.

"Did you get a late start?" my father asked. "You said you'd be back before now."

"I hit traffic," I said.

My nerves were still jangled, but I wasn't about to tell them what had happened. My mother would panic. My father would insist that I go to a brain doctor for a battery of tests. Adam, who was a senior in high school, would lobby hard for full-time custody of my car, which we were supposed to be sharing.

"Well, don't just stand there," my mother said. "Come sit down and eat."

I nodded and took my place at the table. A big serving bowl of spaghetti in meat sauce sat in the center of the table flanked by an even bigger wooden bowl of salad and a basket of crusty garlic bread, one of my all-time favorite foods in the world. I grabbed a piece of garlic bread and chomped down on it. I wasn't that hungry, but I ate anyway, to calm my nerves.

The memory of that incident became my Personal Spark #1.

My second big scare wasn't as dramatic as falling asleep behind the wheel, but in a way it scared me more. Maybe because it was always with me as a constant reminder of the perilous situation I was in.

I had noticed that since high school my ankles had gotten more and more swollen, but I really didn't think anything of it. I'd sit in my favorite chair in the den and put my feet up on the hassock as I snacked and watched TV. Every once in a blue moon during the commercials, I'd notice my ankles and how big they'd become. But by the time the commercials were over and the show came back on, I'd forget about it.

By my second year of college, my ankles had grown to the size of my calves. I didn't seem to have ankles at all anymore, just legs straight down to my shoes. But after my trip to the endocrinologist, I couldn't ignore the state of my ankles. In fact, I became obsessed with them. You see, the doctor had told me that I was at risk for type 2 diabetes. Edema, the abnormal accumulation of fluids beneath the skin, typically in the limbs, is an early warning sign of diabetes, he'd told me.

I remember sitting in the den not long after that trip to the endocrinologist, staring at my ankles up on the hassock. I crossed my leg over my knee as best I could and poked a finger into my ankle. When I removed my finger, the skin didn't bounce back into shape. I stared at the indentation intently. It stayed that way for several minutes. Too many minutes.

I was terrified the first time I saw this, but it soon became like a scab I couldn't stop picking. Whenever I thought about it—and I thought about it a lot—I'd stick my finger into my ankle and wait for the skin to return to normal, hoping that this time it would bounce back a little faster. But it never did. And I never stopped testing it, praying that the next time would be different.

One day when I was back at school, Bill, a guy who lived on my floor, caught me doing this in the lounge.

"Hey," Bill said, startling me. I hadn't noticed him come into the room.

He stared at what I was doing with my ankle. "Man, you can put a belly button on your ankle. Cool."

Well, from my point of view, it wasn't very cool at all.

"Can you do that all over your body?" Bill asked.

I just gave him a look that said, don't go there.

"Sorry," he said. He turned around and left the room.

But getting caught didn't stop me from doing this over and over again, and it was a good thing that I didn't stop because as I continued to do it, the thought of getting diabetes gradually changed from a boogeyman fear to a personal spark. This was something I had to overcome, I told myself. I had to avoid getting diabetes, and the clearest sign that I was out of danger would be when I could stick my finger into my ankle and the skin would bounce back, meaning there was no fluid buildup in there. It became my Personal Spark #2.

Falling asleep at the wheel and driving off the road scared the hell out of me. So did my big fat blobby ankles. I'm not glad that these things happened to me, but ultimately they were good for me. They were the kicks in the butt that told me I needed to do something about my weight problem.

I managed to transform my fears into incentives. I did this by keeping the running-off-the-road incident and my fluid-filled ankles fresh in my mind. When I finally got serious about dieting, there were plenty of times when I got discouraged and thought about throwing in the towel. That's when I would mentally revisit the afternoon I went careening over the grass at sixty miles an hour with Bon Jovi rocking on the radio.

Every time I thought about going down to Burger King for a Whopper and an extra-large order of fries, I summoned the memory of me sitting behind the wheel of my parents' minivan, gripping the wheel for dear life, wondering if this was the end.

Every time I considered a "reward" trip to the Chinese

buffet for sticking to my diet, I recalled the swerving skid marks my tires had made in the grass.

Every time I opened the yellow pages for the Pizza Hut number so I could order a large Meat Lover's for a midnight snack, I closed my eyes and imagined the horrible multi-vehicle accident I could have caused with mangled cars and overturned trailer trucks all over the highway.

Every time I got the hankering for a Big Gulp of regular Coke, instead of Diet Coke, I pictured a school bus lying on its side with a swarm of rescue workers pulling injured kids out of the windows.

And when I wasn't willing to relive that terrible experience on the road, I would just look down at my bloated ankles. I didn't even have to lift my pant legs and stick my finger into my flesh. I knew what was down there, and it reminded me that I didn't want to get diabetes.

These were my personal sparks. Whenever I needed a thought to spur me on or a jolt to prevent me from going back to my old eating habits, I would use them. They were my personal power packs—powerful because they were unique to me, based on my own experiences, and far better than generic warnings about the dangers of obesity. Whenever temptation threatened to lure me back into trouble, my personal sparks kicked in and carried me away to a safer place.

Unfortunately I didn't start using my personal sparks right away. It took a while before I was able to transform these nightmares about diabetes and sleep apnea into positive incentives. I got the big scare from the endocrinologist during winter break of my third year at college, and it wasn't until the middle of spring semester that I got stoked. But by then I was ready to make it happen. The three false starts with the diets that had failed did not discourage me. I kept telling myself that there was something out there that would work for me, something that would make sense to me and that I would stick with. I just had to find it.

And then one day when I wasn't even trying, I did find it. Right next door.

Find Your Personal Spark

- Turn a negative into a positive, or what I call a personal spark. Transform your deepest fear into an incentive—getting arrested for drug possession, for instance—and think of that every time you get the urge to light up a joint.
- Develop a few personal sparks and pull them out whenever you're tempted by your addiction, be it overeating, taking drugs, getting drunk, overspending, whatever.

LESSON 5

One Size Doesn't Fit All

Interstate 95, the highway that runs from the tip of Florida all the way up to the coast of Maine, is traveled by more people than any other road in America. But it won't get you to California.

Chocolate has to be the most popular flavor in the world. But there are some people who don't like chocolate. But what if all of a sudden the only desserts available anywhere were chocolate? They'd be stuck.

If you went to the store to buy a dress and all they sold were clothes in one size and you weren't that size, you'd be out of luck.

The point is, *one size doesn't fit all.*

Well, you're probably thinking, everybody knows that.

In concept, yes, everybody does know that, but when it comes to dealing with big problems, people get roped into thinking that one size *does* fit all.

Read any diet book on the market. Research any commercial diet program you can find. They all have strict rules and regulations. There is little or no room for variation or experimentation. One size fits all. Take it or leave it.

Same thing with twelve-step programs. The underlying message is, follow the steps as prescribed or else you won't succeed. These programs are like the terrible boss who tells his employees, "It's my way or the highway."

"Boot camps" for troubled teens are the obvious extension of these kinds of overbearing philosophies. The message is clear: There is only one solution. This is it. Follow it or fail.

You know what I say to that? Baloney.

You buy clothes to express your uniqueness. You decorate your home to reflect your individual taste. You buy foods that appeal to *you*, not the guy next door. So why would you think that a diet book written for every overweight person in the world would work for little ol' you? It doesn't make sense, does it?

When you're trying to overcome a big problem and change your life, *you must think for yourself.*

Gather as much pertinent information as you can. Check the Internet. Go to the library. Consult bona fide experts. But then analyze the problem for yourself.

Experiment.

Think outside the box.

Create a plan that you think will work for *you* instead of a prepackaged one that's aimed at everyone in general and no one in particular.

You wouldn't buy a dress that's four sizes too big.

You wouldn't buy a chocolate bar if you didn't like chocolate.

You wouldn't take a highway that covered only the East Coast if you were trying to get to the West Coast.

So don't buy into books and programs that aren't right for *you*.

Get the facts and create a strategy that's as unique as you are.

I had tried three different diets, and I'd crashed and burned with all three. Naturally I was frustrated, and what made me feel even worse was that I'd bailed on each one in less than a week.

Initially I'd felt like a failure. I blamed myself. There had to be something wrong with me because I couldn't follow a simple diet and lose weight. Plenty of people did it. Why couldn't I?

But then I thought about it. I had followed these diets to the letter, eaten exactly what I was supposed to, and cut out all the forbidden foods—at least until I gave up. I figured if the diet was any good, it would have encouraged me to stick with it, right? In reality *I* wasn't the one who had failed. It was the *diets* that had failed.

I started searching for another diet. I picked up some books and looked up pertinent articles at the library. As I was doing my research, one thing struck me about all these diets. *They didn't make any sense to me.*

Maybe they had made sense to the people who had succeeded with them, but to me they were ridiculous and in some cases extreme.

Just eat protein.

Just eat one thing a day for every meal.

Just eat fruit.

Just eat rice.

Just drink shakes.

Just eat a certain brand of frozen entrées.

These diets seemed crazy to me. The author of one diet book I read actually recommended carrying a head of raw cabbage around with you and nibbling on it whenever you had a craving. This wasn't a diet for human beings!

I stopped beating myself up about my failures and told myself that in real life *one size doesn't fit all*. I just had to keep searching until I found the diet that was right for me. But I had to do it soon because spring break was coming.

Everyone I knew at school had plans for spring break. If they weren't going home, they were migrating south for warm weather, sunny beaches, and nonstop partying in places like Fort Lauderdale and South Padre Island. Naturally I wasn't going anywhere near a beach, not with the way I felt about my body. And anyway, I couldn't get on a plane—I was too big. Even if they would have let me take two seats, I couldn't afford them. And if I drove to Florida or the Gulf Coast, spring break would be half over by the time I got there.

But I didn't want to go home. Like most college students, I liked the freedom of living on my own, so I decided to stay in Bloomington. I had a small part-time job at a mom-and-pop video rental store, and I asked my boss if I could work more hours that week to fill up my time and make some extra money.

I really liked that job. Even though I was in public view, customers saw me only from the chest up because the checkout counter was that high. And when I wasn't checking out videos, I could sit down and watch movies. My favorites were the comedies. What could be better?

I arrived at work on the Friday before spring break, hoping that Mr. Jenks, my boss, would give me at least thirty hours for the next week. But I was more than a little disappointed when I took a look at my schedule.

"Only eighteen hours?" I said. "I can put in more hours if you need me. Really."

Mr. Jenks pressed his lips into a sympathetic smile and shook his head. "It's gonna be a slow week with all the college kids gone, Jared. I really don't need you for any more than that. Sorry."

"Yeah, I guess you're right," I said.

I went behind the desk and relieved the guy who worked before me. *Beauty and the Beast* was playing on the big TV set bolted to the wall. Mr. Jenks insisted that we play only G-rated movies during the day when parents came in with their kids. I stared blankly at the screen, not really paying attention to what was going on in the movie. Only eighteen hours, I thought glumly. Not good.

It wasn't that I desperately needed the extra money. What I desperately needed was something to do with myself during that week off from school. Me with nothing to do was a very bad combination because when I got bored,

I ate. I could just see myself hanging around the apartment, playing video games, and eating anything I could get my hands on.

As Mr. Jenks had predicted, it was a slow day for a Friday. The exodus had started as kids fled from campus for the break. When *Beauty and the Beast* ended, I picked another G-rated movie from the shelf of approved "daytime" movies. I popped *Toy Story* into the VCR, pressed "play," and let it roll as I continued to obsess about my situation.

Maybe I should find another diet, quick, I thought. I could go over to the big mega-bookstore after work and comb through the diet section again. Maybe some new books had come in. But I wasn't very hopeful. I'd checked out dozens of diet books in the stores, hopeful that I'd find the one that was right for me. But as I said, none of them made any sense to me, and if a diet didn't make any sense, I knew I wasn't going to follow it.

My shift ended at 7:00 P.M., and I dreaded the thought of going back to the apartment. JL had told me that he'd be leaving for home that afternoon. The place was empty, and I'd be alone with the whole evening ahead of me. I could watch TV, read a book, or play video games, but each of those activities would stimulate my appetite by force of habit. There wasn't much food in the apartment, but there was a phone and a phone book. Our apartment was in the "student ghetto," and there were plenty of restaurants, pizzerias, and fast-food places that delivered to our neighborhood. I would be just seven digits away from any high-fat, high-calorie food I desired. I knew myself well enough to know that I might resist temptation for one night but not for a whole week.

I got off the bus on the corner in front of my building, feeling alone and vulnerable. The apartment building was three stories high and nearly a block long. A couple of girls who lived on the second floor were packing up a red VW Beetle parked at the curb, giddy and excited about wherever they were going. I didn't want to walk by them. At the beginning of the semester, I'd heard one of them laughing and making fun of me as I passed by. I wasn't in the mood for a repeat.

It was dinnertime, and I was feeling hungry. I hadn't even thought about what I would do for dinner, but I was determined not to call out for takeout. Even if I ordered something healthy the first time, I felt that it would open the door for more takeout, and I knew how I was—it wouldn't be long before I was ordering midnight pizzas.

Fortunately there was a Subway sandwich shop right in the building. It was on the corner near the bus stop. Two apartments on the first floor had been gutted to make way for the restaurant, and I have to admit it was part of the reason why I picked that building. Who needed to shop when you had a fast-food restaurant just a few doors down?

The girls were taking their time loading the Beetle, so I decided to go into the Subway and get a sandwich for dinner. For some reason they were busy that night. Seven people were standing in line ahead of me. I didn't like having to wait, but at least it would keep me out of the apartment for a little while longer.

I overheard the woman at the head of the line ordering several sandwiches. Must be buying dinner for her whole family, I figured. I heaved a sigh, sensing that this was going to take a while. I wished I had brought something to read with me.

I looked around for the free newspapers that usually sat in a pile by the front door, but something else caught my eye instead—a bunch of pamphlets in a rack on the wall. I took a closer look and read the title on the cover: SUBWAY NUTRITIONAL AND DIETARY GUIDE: 7 UNDER 6.

I wondered what that meant, "7 under 6." I went over to the rack, took a pamphlet, and got back into line. I started reading. "7 under 6," I discovered, referred to seven different Subway sandwiches that contained 6 grams of fat or less.

Hmmm, I thought. From my diet book reading, I knew that a meal with fewer than 6 grams of fat was pretty good. I opened the pamphlet and read more.

The pamphlet was made up mostly of charts that showed the stats on everything they served in the restaurant, the same way packaged foods in the supermarket show their nutritional content on the boxes and labels. The Subway charts even gave values separately for what went into the sandwiches, including the bread, cheese, mayo, mustard, and oil. It also gave similar breakdowns for all the chips and desserts they served. I was impressed that the company would go to the trouble to print this information in a pamphlet for their customers. I couldn't think of any other fast-food restaurants that did that.

I glanced up and noticed that the woman with the big order was at the cash register paying for her sandwiches. There were still six other people ahead of me, so I went back to the pamphlet.

I checked the values on some of my favorite sandwiches, and I was shocked. An Italian BMT is 450 calories with 21 grams of total fat. And that was just for the 6-inch sandwich, not the 12-inch, which is what I always ordered. Whoa!

The pamphlet included a chart that contained some of Subway's competitors' offerings. A Big Mac contains 600 calories and 33 grams of fat. A Whopper has 700 calories and 42 grams of fat. Jeez, I thought. It wasn't unusual for me to gobble down a half dozen of these burgers in a day.

I flipped back to the first chart in the pamphlet, the "7 under 6" chart. I scanned the calorie column and discovered that a 6-inch turkey sandwich has just 280 calories and 4.5 grams of fat. The 6-inch Veggie Delite sandwich has 230 calories and 3 grams of fat.

Interesting, I thought.

I went to the chips chart and discovered that a small bag of baked potato chips has 130 calories and 1.5 grams of fat.

I did a little quick math in my head. Say I had a 6-inch turkey sub, a bag of baked chips, and a diet soda for lunch and a 12-inch Veggie Delite with baked chips and a diet soda for dinner, I would have consumed a little more than a thousand calories. And they'd be low-fat calories. And if

I had just a cup of coffee for breakfast, I'd be way under the 2,000 calories a day recommended for a person my age and height.

It sounded too good to be true, so I ran the numbers again. But my addition had been right the first time.

A lightbulb flashed in my head.

This could be the solution I'd been looking for. A little over 1,000 calories a day eating food I actually liked. I had never tried the Veggie Delite sandwich, but I had eaten Subway's turkey sandwiches before—loaded with extra cheese and mayo at my request, of course. But no more of that. I was psyched.

Plus, it was convenient. Healthy food was just a few steps from where I lived.

It just didn't seem possible that this would work, but the more I thought about it, the more possible it seemed. Finally I had found something that really made sense to me.

But wait a minute, I thought. This is crazy. Look at that bread.

I peered through the glass counter at the plump loaves of white and wheat bread on display. How could I possibly lose weight eating bread like that? Bread was fattening, right?

I loved bread, and bread was part of the reason I'd gotten so heavy. When I was a kid and my family would go out to a restaurant for dinner, I'd make sure I ordered something reasonable from the menu so that my parents wouldn't get on my case about my poor eating habits. But my focus would be on the bread basket. I'd gradually nibble away on dinner roll after dinner roll until the basket

was empty, then pray that the waitress would bring us another one, which is usually what happened. I can remember many occasions when I polished off nearly two baskets
of bread and butter, and nobody at the table—not my parents, my brother, or my sister—was any wiser.

So in my mind bread was a bad thing. A diet that included 18 inches worth of bread a day could never work. I
checked the pamphlet to see what it had to say about that,
and to my amazement the values given for the sandwiches
included the bread.

Damn, I thought. This really could work.

"Next. Next! Sir, can I help you?"

I looked up from the pamphlet. The girl behind the
counter was talking to me. She was waiting for me to place
my order. I'd been so deep in thought, I didn't even realize
that I was at the front of the line.

"Uh . . ." I scanned the menu board on the wall over
her head. I usually ordered a 12-inch steak and cheese
sandwich with extra meat and cheese and plenty of mayo.

"What can I get you?" the girl asked.

I was at a crossroads. I could try something new or fall
back into my old, bad, comforting eating habits.

"Sir? There are other people waiting."

"I know. I'm sorry," I said. "I . . ."

It was now or never. Just do it, I told myself. Try it.

"I want a 6-inch turkey sub on whole wheat," I said,
gripping the pamphlet tightly.

"What kind of cheese?" she asked.

"No cheese, thank you."

"You got it."

She assembled my sandwich and passed it on to the next person behind the counter, a young man. "What would you like on it?" he asked. "Mayo? Mustard? Oil and vinegar—"

"Mustard," I said, cutting him off before he tempted me with a creamy dressing. "Spicy mustard."

"Lettuce, tomato, onions, green peppers, sweet peppers, jalapeños, olives?"

"Ah . . . everything except tomatoes, onions, and olives, please."

He put the fixings on my sandwich. "For here or to go?" he asked.

"To go."

He wrapped it up and passed it on to the young woman at the cash register. "Anything else?" she asked.

"Yes," I said. "A small bag of potato chips—the baked kind—and a large soda."

She rang me up and handed me a large cup. I paid her and went to the soda dispensers. I usually filled up with regular Coke and not too much ice, but this time I took a little more ice and chose Diet Coke instead. I stuck the pamphlet in my back pocket and headed home. I wanted to read more about the Subway stats.

The two ditzy girls from upstairs were still loading up their Beetle, but I hardly gave them a second look as I passed by. I wanted to taste this sandwich, see if I liked it as much as what I usually ordered. I wanted to find out what a low-fat, low-calorie fast-food meal was like. I wanted to like it. I *desperately* wanted to like it.

As soon as I got back to my apartment, I sat down at the kitchen table, unwrapped my sub, and took a big bite. It wasn't bad. In fact it was good, *very* good. It wasn't an overstuffed cheese steak with gobs of mayonnaise, but it was good. I glanced at the refrigerator and remembered the terrible low-cal frozen entrées and the awful shakes I'd tried. By comparison, this sandwich was heavenly.

I opened the bag of chips and chomped down on one. Not as greasy as regular chips. They were different than what I was used to, but they weren't bad.

I stuck a straw in my soda and took a sip. Same thing here. The taste of Diet Coke wasn't what I was used to, but I could live with it.

I bit into my sandwich and finished it off in no time. I had always been a fast eater, probably because my dad is a fast eater, and when I was a little kid, I feared that he'd finish his portion and then eat mine. I ate the last of the chips and shook the crumbs in the bag directly into my mouth. I sucked up the last drops of my soda, and the loud slurping sound filled the apartment. Suddenly I realized how quiet it was with everyone gone. On most nights the faint sounds of stereos and TVs and people talking in other apartments carried through the thin walls. I'd never thought about it before, but the sounds of other people were sort of comforting, a gentle reminder that I wasn't alone in the complex, or the world. But with everyone gone for spring break, the place was silent.

I crumpled up the sandwich wrapper and the potato-chip bag and threw them in the trash. The clock on the stove showed the time in a green digital glow: 8:18.

Now what am I supposed to do? I wondered. I had the rest of the night ahead of me.

I picked up the soda cup, brought the straw to my mouth, and tried to suck up a little more, but it was just ice. I dumped it in the sink and threw out the cup. I noticed the phone book sitting on the counter.

I didn't really feel full. Should've ordered a 12-inch, I thought.

Tomorrow night, I told myself. I'll get the big one to-morrow night.

I pulled the Subway pamphlet out of my back pocket and flipped through it, scanning the charts, rereading the calorie and fat counts. This could work, I thought. Two sandwiches a day, two bags of chips, two sodas. This really could work.

I looked around the empty apartment, listening to the silence. My eye drifted back to the yellow pages on the counter. My stomach rumbled. I sighed.

It was going to be a long night.

One Size Doesn't Fit All

- When you're trying to overcome a big problem and change your life, you must think for yourself. Don't depend on someone else's method.
- No single program for change works for everyone because each person is a unique individual. Find the one that will work for you.

- If a program for change is going to work, it has to make sense to you. If it doesn't, you will never follow it.
- If you can't find a method that works for you, create your own.

Change Your Mind to Change Your Life

We've all heard the expression, "If life gives you lemons, make lemonade."

A variation on the theme is, "If you can't hide it, highlight it."

In other words, take what you've got and do something positive with it.

You can use this attitude to defeat whatever problem is holding your life hostage. But to make this transformation, you'll have to change your ingrained notions about the things that are affecting you.

Overweight people, for instance, are afraid of being hungry. Hunger is not a comfortable feeling, therefore they think hunger is bad and possibly even harmful. But that's a preconceived notion and an erroneous one.

You can turn that negative notion on its head and make it a tool for losing weight. Just tell yourself that hunger is good, that it's concrete proof that you're losing weight. Don't think of it as your body's desperate cry for nourishment. Think of it as a compliment from your body, a pat on the back, a high five for the progress you're making.

Shopoholics want things that they don't need. Nevertheless, that feeling of want and need takes over their personalities. They become obsessed with making purchases, often buying things that they can't afford. It takes over their lives and can lead to financial ruin. Shopoholics can't cope with their impulses. Their desire to spend becomes a vicious beast, and they come to feel that the beast must be fed every time it growls.

But who says so? Why not just let the beast growl? Make the craving to spend a good thing. Welcome it. See it as a positive indication that you're dealing with your problem.

Turn your obsession around and make it work for you. Sucking it up and enduring the desire to spend means that the shopoholic is saving money. It means that he's not being wasteful. It also means that he isn't cluttering his house with unnecessary purchases. All positives.

People with substance addictions—whether it's caffeine, nicotine, alcohol, or narcotics—go through withdrawal when they don't get what their bodies have come to crave. I don't take these kinds of addictions lightly, and I'm not suggesting that withdrawal can be managed easily or without the help of medical professionals, but changing your mind about withdrawal can make a big difference.

If a person thinks of physical withdrawal as harmful and dangerous, she'll run right back to her drug of choice to avoid the pain and anguish. But if that person thinks of withdrawal as a sign of *progress* in the battle against her addiction, perhaps she won't dread it quite as much. She can think of it as a symptom of the body undergoing a change for the better.

When I was trying to lose weight, I constantly compared the tastes of low-calorie, low-fat foods with the high-calorie, high-fat foods I knew and loved. I felt that diet sodas had a chemical aftertaste. Baked potato chips were just okay and not nearly as satisfying as the salty, greasy, regular chips. I didn't dislike the taste of mustard on my sandwiches, but I didn't like it as much as mayonnaise. And I loved cheese. All my life I had thought of it as a necessary ingredient on a sandwich. In fact, I couldn't imagine a sandwich without cheese—ham and American cheese, turkey and Swiss, Italian cold cuts and provolone, cheesesteaks. Well, there is no law that says a sandwich has to have cheese, and I learned that very tasty sandwiches can be made without it.

When I got serious about losing weight, all my preconceived notions about food had to change. I had to change my mind about low-calorie, low-fat foods and learn how to live with them. Every time I encountered a diet taste that was different from what I was used to or that I didn't particularly care for, I told myself that it was an indication of the calories I *wasn't* putting into my body. And that's a positive.

I was also able to "trick" myself into eating better by eating a fast food that was healthy. I was hopelessly addicted to fast food, but in Subway sandwiches I found a fast food that satisfied my psychological as well as my physical cravings.

Your brain leads your body, so in order to make a change in your life, change your mind first.

If you've seen me on the Subway television commercials, holding up my "fat pants," you might have gotten the impression that Subway sandwiches were my magic pill for weight loss, that after I'd discovered the health benefits of their low-calorie, low-fat sandwiches, it was a straight and easy path to dramatic weight loss. If that's what you think, let me set the record straight.

There is no straight and easy path to dramatic weight loss.

There is no straight and easy path to any major life change.

I am not exaggerating when I say that the night I had my first healthy Subway sandwich was a dark night of the soul for me. Not long after I ate that sandwich, my old demons converged on me, haunting me and tempting me to eat more. They were hard to resist.

When the hunger pangs started, I went to my computer and surfed the Net for more information about weight loss and the truth about foods that seem to be healthy but really aren't. I wanted to make sure that anything I put on my sandwiches from now on wouldn't undermine my efforts. For instance, I had always thought of cheese as dairy and thus basically a good food, but I found out that most cheeses are high in fat. What really surprised me was that olive oil, which I'd always heard was the healthy oil, was in reality loaded with fat and had every bit as many calories as butter. I resolved not to put either of these items on my sandwiches in the future.

Of course, reading about cheese made me hungry for cheese. Cheddar cheese, American cheese, Swiss cheese, mozzarella cheese, all kinds of cheeses. And reading about olive oil reminded me of Italian food, and my stomach groaned longingly for pasta and meatballs and lasagna and veal parmesan and my all-time favorite, garlic bread.

Almost every Web site on nutrition featured pictures of food, and that made me hungry, too. I looked over my shoulder toward the kitchen. The yellow pages on the counter started calling to me: "Don't make yourself miserable, Jared. Order a pizza."

I logged off and shut down the computer. I didn't want to see any more pictures of food.

My stomach rumbled, pleading with me. It wanted a pizza, extra large, extra cheese, three meat toppings.

I tried to ignore the temptations and plopped down in front of the TV. I channel-surfed until I found a movie that looked interesting, a Civil War epic. I started getting into it and watched for a while—until the battle scenes ended and the characters went to a sumptuous Southern dinner on a plantation.

My stomach begged for mercy.

I changed the channel, quickly bypassing all food and

restaurant commercials. I had never realized how many there were until I tried to avoid them. They were like squadrons of vampire bats bombarding me in the night.

I kept flipping channels, working my thumb over the remote. Finally I found a stand-up comic doing his routine in front of an audience. He was actually pretty funny and his jokes took my mind off eating—until he started in on airline food.

Click!

A romantic comedy about a couple who keep breaking up and getting back together turned sour for me when the couple made a date to meet at a their favorite restaurant.

Click!

The eleven o'clock news. Great. I'd catch up on the events of the day. Votes in congress. The president making a speech. A three-alarm fire at a local factory, which totally destroyed the entire building. The weather forecast. Sports. And finally a human-interest piece on a blueberry pie–eating contest, featuring a line of big-bellied contestants, their faces smeared purple.

Click!

A martial arts movie. Young villagers training with a kung-fu master to defend their village from invaders. Terrific. That had to be safe, I thought. And it was—until the students took a much-deserved break from their grueling training regimen for a meal of rice and vegetables prepared by the master who regaled them with advice about the value of a good, hearty meal.

Click! Click! Click!

I channel-surfed for another hour, bored, disgruntled, and most of all *hungry*! Hunger pangs gnawed at me, and my stomach just wouldn't shut up, like an annoying, whiny toddler who refused to settle down.

I shut off the TV and glanced through the doorway into the kitchen. The yellow pages were in there, waiting. So was the phone. Not that I didn't already know the local pizzeria's number by heart. I checked my watch. It wasn't midnight yet. They stayed open late and delivered. I still had time.

But I didn't get out of my chair. I didn't want to do it. I didn't want to give in to temptation.

Get up, my stomach urged. *Make the call, Jared. Order a pizza. I know you want one. We both want one.*

Well, there was no question about that. Midnight pizzas had become a habit with me. My body had gotten used to a load of carbs and fat before bed. It was crying out for its nightly fix. If I had ever doubted that overeating was an addiction, I was totally convinced now.

My stomach made the loudest, most pathetic rumble I'd ever heard, and I'd heard it make all kinds of noises in the past.

But I resisted. I told myself it was just begging for sympathy. At 425 pounds I was hardly in danger of starving. And more than anything, I didn't want to fail again.

My stomach rumbled again, even more pathetic this time.

I ignored the moaning and groaning and headed for the bathroom. I washed my face, brushed my teeth, took off my clothes, and crawled into bed. I figured sleep was the only solution at this point. If I was asleep, I couldn't eat.

But my stomach was insistent. It kept me up for quite a while, prodding me with hunger pangs that just wouldn't quit. I'm not sure if I just got used to the feeling or my stomach finally gave up, but I eventually fell asleep.

The next morning I woke up hungry but, surprisingly, not ravenous. And the fact that I wasn't ravenous kept me from jumping in the car and going out to IHOP for a jumbo stack of pancakes with lots of butter and my choice of syrup with a double side order of bacon, ham, and sausage. Instead, I kept to the plan and fixed myself a cup of coffee. That's all.

As you might suspect, my stomach wasn't happy. As soon as I finished my coffee, it started rumbling and grumbling again. I looked at my watch. It was just about nine o'clock. I had to wait at least three hours before I could have lunch. And I wasn't scheduled to work until three that day. I had a whole morning and part of the afternoon to fill. I was in a perilous overeating danger zone.

But I remained determined. Remember, I was always motivated whenever I *started* a new diet, and this time was no exception. I was not going to snack and cheat at this stage of the game. Besides, I was curious to see if my experiment with low-fat, low-cal Subway sandwiches would work.

I decided to go out and stay out until it was time for lunch. I went to the front window to see what the weather was like, and my heart sank. There was frost on the windowpane. It was still winter in Indiana, and we'd had another freeze overnight. This kind of weather always filled me with dread.

I had come to hate winter, but not for the usual reasons.

I was afraid of ice. Ice was my enemy. At my weight my balance was iffy at best. Whenever it got this cold, I always feared that I would slip on the ice and fall. And that would be bad news for me.

For one thing, getting back on my feet would be a major chore, and I might even have to ask for help. How humiliating would that be? Me on my belly struggling to get to my knees, hollering for somebody to come help me up. I could just imagine those two nasty girls from upstairs pointing at me and laughing their heads off.

But the scenario I feared even more was falling down and hurting myself, breaking a bone, maybe a leg. I had nightmares that I would be confined to a wheelchair. And what kind of wheelchair would they get for me? The Hummer of wheelchairs? And would the damaged bone ever be able to support my weight again? I could end up being a cripple.

I moved away from the window and turned on the TV to check the local weather forecast. Fortunately it called for sunny skies and temperatures above freezing by noon. That was good. But I still had to fill up my morning with something besides eating.

My stomach grumbled insidiously, as if it were confident that I would eventually succumb to temptation. Trapped in the house with nothing good on TV at this hour and just video games and the Internet to occupy me, I would surely scavenge the kitchen and eat anything I could find. And knowing me, I would eat all of it.

I furrowed my brow and frowned. This was bad. I looked

out the window again, hoping for the sun to burn through the clouds, but my wish was not the sun's command.

My stomach emitted a rippling rumble as if it were laughing at me.

I sat down in my armchair in front of the television. The remote was on the coffee table within reach. I imagined commercials for all kinds of foods. I imagined cooking shows and morning talk shows with cooking segments. They would all trigger my appetite. I decided not to watch television.

My stomach made a new noise, smaller than a rumble, more like a burble. It was almost funny, and it made me smile.

And that's when something occurred to me.

Up until this point I had been thinking of these hunger pangs as a bad thing. But in reality what were they? Nothing. They weren't signs of distress or illness. I definitely wasn't on the verge of starvation. These stomach noises were just an indication that I was changing my bad eating habits. And so, I thought, they were really a *good* thing.

From that moment I started to think of my rumbles and pangs as *rewards*. I viewed them as *positive feedback from my body* that I was doing the right thing.

I visualized each pang and rumble as a little chunk of fat inside me melting away like an ice cube on a hot skillet. My stomach grumbling was the sound of me getting thinner. The gnawing feeling of a hunger pang was the sensation of my body fat being rendered and dripping away.

And as far as falling into the video game/Internet surfing/snacking trap, I foiled my smart-aleck stomach by picking up a book and starting to read. It was something that JL had recommended to me a while ago, Stephen King's *It*. I got into it after only a few pages and would have been totally engrossed if it weren't for my pangs and rumblings.

But that was okay. I grinned a little each time my stomach interrupted my reading. The fat was disappearing, I told myself.

At twelve o'clock sharp, I put down the book, left my apartment, and headed over to the Subway sandwich shop. Once again I ordered a 6-inch turkey sub on whole wheat with mustard and lots of veggies (except for tomatoes, onions, and olives, which I don't like). I had a small bag of baked potato chips and a large diet soda to go with the sandwich.

It was a satisfying lunch, but around about two o'clock my stomach started protesting again. I didn't like the feeling at first, but I kept on telling myself that it was a sign that I was beginning to lose weight. My rumbling stomach constantly reminded me that good things were happening to my body, and that kept me from sneaking off for a half-dozen tacos or a double-patty burger with fries and a vanilla shake.

I stuck it out and endured the hunger pangs all through my shift at the video store, which wasn't easy, considering that I was trying to go from massive overeating to sensible eating in just one day. At seven o'clock I went back to Subway for a 12-inch Veggie Delite sandwich. I ordered another bag of baked chips and a large diet soda to wash it down. As I walked back to my apartment with my dinner, I doubted that a vegetable sandwich would be enough food for me.

But, happily, I was wrong. I was surprised at how much I liked the Veggie Delite. It was plenty of food, essentially a large, fresh salad—your choice of lettuce, tomatoes, red onions, green peppers, pickles, and olives—on a sandwich roll slathered with mustard.

Afterward, I watched some TV and played video games for a while, and eventually my stomach started rumbling again. I was tempted to go foraging in the kitchen cabinets, but I was determined to break my old snacking habits, so I pulled myself away from the computer and went back to the book I'd started reading that morning.

Every few minutes my stomach would remind me that we were hungry, but instead of getting alarmed, I just ignored it and kept on reading.

Things were happening, I told myself. Good things.

Change Your Mind to Change Your Life

- Turn your addiction around and make it work for you. Think of the pain and discomfort of withdrawal as positive feedback that you're kicking your habit. Hunger pangs, for instance, indicate that you're not putting excess calories into your body. Your grumbling stomach is telling you that you're losing weight.

- Get used to new tastes and sensations. Many people say they can't stand the taste of diet soda, for instance, but in reality it's not bad, just different. It's what you're going to have to live with if you intend to lose weight and keep it off.
- The brain leads the body. To change your life, change your mind first.

Don't Tell Anyone

You always need the support of family and friends when you're trying to make a big change in your life. Medical professionals, therapists, clergy, personal trainers, tutors, and loved ones can provide invaluable help in achieving your goal. But if you tell too many people what you're doing, they will expect to see signs of progress, and this creates unnecessary pressure.

Remember, you're making this change for *you*, not for them. The strength you need to reach your goal can't come from them. Ultimately you must find your own inner strength to move forward.

I had failed at dieting many times, and each time the people who knew I was dieting became disappointed or jaded.

"I'm sorry you didn't lose any weight on that diet, Jared. But don't worry. You'll find one that'll work for you."

Hearing something like that made me want to crawl into bed and cover my head with a blanket.

But even worse than that were the likely comments I didn't hear:

"I wonder how long *this* diet will last."

"Why doesn't he just give up? He's never going to lose weight."

"Poor Jared. He's so clueless."

I didn't have to hear people say these things. Their feelings were clear enough in their expressions and attitudes whenever they were around me.

Sometimes even your most loyal supporters will inadvertently say something that throws you off track. A careless comment or a statement that could be interpreted two ways will prey on your mind and set you back.

No matter what you're trying to do—lose weight, break a bad habit, kick a dependency—you're doing it for yourself and no one else. Therefore, you have to do it yourself. You have to provide your own personal motivation.

Imagine what would have happened if I had announced that my new diet plan consisted of Subway sandwiches, chips, and soda. People would have laughed at me. My family would have tried to have me committed.

But I had done my homework. The numbers didn't lie, so I knew, at least in theory, this could work. But I also knew that I had to do it quietly. I didn't dare tell anyone. I couldn't bear the disappointment of another failure and the criticism that would follow.

When you've made up your mind that you're going to

change your life, don't tell anyone. It'll be that much sweeter when you succeed.

When I started my self-styled Subway sandwich diet, I didn't tell *anyone* what I was doing. With all my other diets, even the ones I'd tried in high school, my friends and family knew that I was dieting, and when I inevitably failed, they were disappointed, and their disappointment made me feel terrible. I felt that I had failed and let them down. And that made it more difficult for me to start a new diet. Eventually my unsuccessful attempts at dieting became so predictable, I became like the boy who cried wolf. Whenever I announced that I was starting a new diet, nobody really believed that I would stick to it, even if they didn't come right out and say so out loud to me.

Nothing was more embarrassing to me than being asked about my dieting and having to admit that I had failed. Every year my extended family has a big reunion dinner, a dress-up, sit-down affair usually held at a country club. The dinner always happens in early September, and it's a family tradition with all my aunts, uncles, and cousins gathering together, easily more than a hundred people. There's always plenty of food, not all of it healthy, especially the desserts.

When I was a little kid, I always looked forward to these reunions. It was an opportunity to pig out without my parents getting on my case. But as I got heavier, I started to dread these get-togethers. They became Let's-See-How-Fat-Jared-Got-This-Year Day. Many of the relatives who attended didn't live close by, and we didn't see them that often. I could sense them staring at me behind my back, comparing me to their memories of the last time they saw me, clucking their tongues in pity or disapproval.

Most people deal with obese individuals by not dealing with them at all. They look away and avoid eye contact. They treat the person as if he's invisible. But let me tell you from experience: This kind of treatment is worse than having someone shout out, "Hey, fatso!" At least an insult acknowledges that you're there. Avoiding the obese person makes him or her feel like a zero—worthless.

Several members of my family would habitually give me the cloak of invisibility at these reunions, but not my grandfather on my mother's side. One of the things I love about my grandpa is his honesty.

I remember one reunion when I was in junior high. Grandpa was standing by himself, digging into a generous slice of apple pie à la mode that threatened to slide off his plate. He had normal weight for a man his age. I walked over to him with a glass of cola in my hand.

"Hey, Grandpa," I said, genuinely glad to see him.

He looked up and smiled. He always had a smile for me. "How've you been, Jared?"

"Okay." I took a sip of my soda.

"How's that diet going? Still doing it?"

I abruptly stopped drinking, and the fizz went right up my nose. I started coughing. When I finally stopped, I could see that Grandpa was still waiting for an answer.

He dug his fork into his pie and shoveled a piece into his mouth. "So you still dieting?" he asked again.

I cringed inside. This was the last question in the world I wanted to hear. "Nope," I said flatly. "Didn't work."

"Oh," he said, nodding as he chewed. "Well, one of these days you'll find a good one. Don't worry."

He could be blunt sometimes, but at least he acknowledged that I was a person and treated me like a human being. I knew deep down he really cared about me.

My parents cared about me, too, but that caring sometimes turned into head-butting. My mom is less confrontational than my dad. She would fret about my weight. My dad was the one who'd sit me down and try to give me the reality check. I remember having to endure a lot of tense heart-to-hearts with him, but one time in particular sticks in my mind. I was in fifth grade, and I probably weighed more than 200 pounds. He sat on one side of the sofa. I sat on the other.

"Jared," my dad said to me, "do you realize what you're doing to yourself? Do you realize that you're ruining your health?"

I just sat there with my arms crossed and sulked. I didn't want to hear it.

"Jared, you have to listen to me. This is important. You have to cut down on what you're eating. Carrying this much weight is bad for you."

I looked up at the ceiling.

He exhaled in frustration. "I'm only telling you this because I care about you. I care about what's going to happen to you if you keep eating this way. I want you to cut way down on the snacks. No more sneaking out for Big Macs. No more extra lunches. No more—"

That's when I figured out a foolproof way to shut him down. I tucked in my chin and pressed it to my chest as hard as I could so that I had a triple chin.

His face turned red, and his eye bulged. He was furious. "Stop that!" he ordered.

But I didn't. I just did it more, squeezing harder, trying to make myself even more grotesque.

"Don't do that!" he yelled.

But I didn't stop. It was my way of defying him, wordlessly telling him that I was fat and I didn't care, just leave me alone.

Looking back, I regret having been so willful and stubborn when all he was trying to do was help me.

As I was growing up (and growing bigger), my weight was not a topic I ever wanted to discuss. I didn't want to share my feelings, and I didn't like probing questions. I didn't want anyone's sympathy or advice, which everyone seemed eager to offer. But at least one person in my family didn't fall into that category: my brother, Adam. We'd had a more contentious relationship growing up, especially when we were both in high school.

Adam is two years younger than me. He's a good-looking guy, and in high school he was popular and got a lot of attention. But he was also known for being the little brother of Jared the blimp. A lot of his friends wondered out loud how he turned out so normal when he shared genes with Jabba the Hut.

At the time I thought of him as a cool and sometimes not-so-nice kid, but looking back, it couldn't have been easy for him having an obese older brother. A lot of his friends had older brothers who kind of showed them the ropes in life. They learned sports from their older brothers. They also learned how to cope with the unpredictable social scene in high school. Adam didn't get much help from me in those areas. I didn't play sports, and I didn't socialize with anyone in high school except for JL. I avoided people as much as I could and spent as little time at school as possible. I wasn't much of a role model for Adam.

After graduating from high school, Adam followed me to Indiana University. Even though we were on the same campus, we didn't see much of each other during the school year. He had his friends and his scene, and I was busy trying to deal with my studies and my weight. I suppose he didn't want to repeat his high school experience and become known as the fat guy's brother.

But there was one thing we did share at school: a car.

My beloved red 1993 Honda Civic hatchback. Even though it was a tight squeeze for me, I loved that car. When I had first gotten my driver's license, my father promised to get me any car I wanted if I started losing weight. Well, that didn't happen, so my dad modified his offer. I didn't have to lose weight to get a car; I only had to choose between a larger used car and a smaller new one. This might have been his way of enticing me to lose weight, thinking that I'd prefer a hot little new car to some big old family sedan. He probably thought that I'd lose weight in order to be more comfortable in a smaller car. I wish it had worked out that way, but it didn't.

Maybe it was because I found the Civic perfectly comfortable despite my size. A lot of it had to do with the moveable steering wheel, which I raised as high as it would go to accommodate my gut.

When I went away to college, the car stayed home because first-year students weren't allowed to keep cars on campus, and the little red Civic went to my brother, who had just gotten his license. While I was away, Adam managed to wreck it, totaled it, completely beyond repair. He wasn't hurt in the accident, but my beloved little car was D.O.A.

I wasn't angry when I got the news. I was just happy that he hadn't gotten hurt. But what did upset me later on was the car that Adam and my father had picked out to replace it. A gold Toyota Corolla. I went home for a weekend and got my first look at the new car. The plan was that Adam would use it while he was in high school, then the two of us would share it when he started college in the fall. I would be in charge of it since I was an upperclassman and allowed to keep a car at school, but he would be able to use it whenever he needed it. We'd also drive home together for vacations.

I went home for the weekend shortly after they'd bought the new car. I arrived on Friday afternoon and sat in the living room, chatting with my mom, eagerly waiting for Adam to get back from school so I could see the new Toyota. As soon as I heard him pulling into the driveway, I went outside to check it out. As I came down the front walk, Adam got out of the car and slammed the door closed.

"So what do you think?" he asked. It was obvious that he was proud of the car and thought of it as his and his alone.

I walked all around the car and gave it the once-over. It looked fine to me. I opened the driver's door, pushed the seat back all the way, and lowered myself in. The steering wheel dug painfully into my belly. I reached for the lever on the steering column to adjust the wheel to tilt it up, but the lever wasn't in the same spot as it had been on the Civic. I felt all around the column, searching for the lever.

I looked up at Adam, who was standing next to the open door. "Where's the steering-wheel tilt?" I asked him.

"This car doesn't have one," he said.

"What?"

"It doesn't have one."

I was flabbergasted and absolutely furious. How could my father let my numbskull brother pick out a car that didn't have an adjustable steering wheel? I instantly assumed that Adam had done this on purpose.

"We have to get rid of this car," I said. "I can't drive it."

"Are you crazy? We're not getting rid of it," Adam said. "There's nothing wrong with it."

I snapped at him. "I can't drive it. Can't you see that?"

He handed me the keys. "Before you start having a hissy fit, try it."

I snatched the keys out of his hand and turned on the engine. I squirmed and fidgeted, trying to get comfortable, but it was impossible. I adjusted the mirrors and fought to get the seat belt buckled. Finally I put the transmission into reverse and backed out of the driveway. The engine had a nice new-car hum, and I could feel that it was peppy, but as I turned the steering wheel to back out into the street, I was very unhappy with the wheel rubbing against my belly. I straightened the car and shifted into drive.

"Hey, wait up," Adam called out. He ran to the passenger side and got in with me.

I glared at him. "Afraid I'll wreck *your* car?"

"You don't want me to come? Fine."

But I was already driving down the street. "Just shut up," I said.

I drove around the neighborhood, and every time I turned a corner, the steering wheel sawed into my flesh. It wasn't painful, but it was annoying. A constant reminder of my size.

"I don't like it," I said. "We need to trade it in and get something else."

"Why?" Adam whined. "It's a good car. I like it."

"We're gonna be sharing it next year," I reminded him. "We need something I can drive."

"Come on, Jared. You only use the car to buy fast food."

I slammed on the brakes, and the car screeched to a halt. I turned my head and stared daggers at him. That really stung. "I use the car for a lot of things," I said. "Not just that."

"Yeah, sure," he grumbled.

We drove home in stony silence. I figured I'd straighten this out directly with my father at dinner that night.

The whole family sat around the dinner table that evening—my parents, my brother, my little sister, Jessica, and me. My mother had made roast beef, mashed potatoes, and peas. I waited until everyone was eating before I broached the topic.

"Hey, Dad, what do you think about trading in the new car and getting another Civic like the old one? That was a much better car than this one." I didn't want to come right out and say that I didn't fit in the new one.

My dad shook his head as he chewed.

"It's a brand-new car, Jared. Just a couple of months old. Given the way new cars depreciate in value, we'd be losing money if we sold it now."

Adam chimed in with his two cents' worth. "You don't want Dad to lose money, do you?"

I just glared at him. They were right, of course, but this wasn't what I wanted to hear. I wanted a car I could fit into.

"I'm sure you can make do with this one, Jared," my mom said.

I kept my mouth shut. If I pressed my point, I knew that this would lead to a discussion about my weight, and I just didn't want to go there. I *never* wanted to go there.

So that we wouldn't argue about the car, my mother diplomatically changed the subject by asking Adam something about his upcoming prom.

I stared down at the roast beef and mashed potatoes in my plate and sulked.

My sister, Jessica, stopped eating and looked at me with sympathy in her eyes. I worked up a smile for her and cut into my roast beef. I didn't want her to be upset, even though inside I was broiling.

The subject was never brought up again. We kept the Corolla, and I learned to live with the discomfort.

My sister and I were always more on the same wavelength, even though she's seven years younger than I am. We bonded because we spent a lot of time together, watching TV and playing video games. Unlike my brother, who was always out doing something, Jessica came straight home after school. I did the same thing because I didn't want to deal with people who might criticize or ridicule me because of my weight. I can remember plenty of afternoons when Jessica and I hung out together in the den, watching TV before we settled down to do our homework. We'd also snack together.

Jessica was a little chubby as a kid, and she liked to eat. Thankfully she never got like me, and now she's a normal weight for her height. But back when we were kids, it was nothing for us to polish off a jumbo bag of chips and a liter of soda while watching a couple of sitcoms. I consumed most of it, of course.

I remember one spring day during my senior year when I decided to treat Jessica to a day at an amusement park, just the two of us. Old Indiana Fun Park was just a forty-minute drive from my parents' house in Indianapolis. It's closed now, but it had been a small, manageable theme park. At the time all-day passes cost only fifteen dollars. I bought one for each of us and looked forward to riding all the rides, something I hadn't done in years.

The day started out great. The first ride we took was the Log Flume, which is like a roller coaster that slices through the water at the end of the ride. The cars resemble huge pine logs and have room for eight passengers.

I loved rides when I was a little kid, and I couldn't wait to get on. As we stood in line, my sister and I agreed that we would do our best to get seats in the front for the maximum thrill. The line advanced, and we got very excited when the ride attendant put up the chain barrier right in front of us. When the next car came, we'd be first in line to get the front seats.

"As soon as he lets us through," I said to my sister, "you run over and take the front seat, okay?"

"Okay!" she said, bouncing with anticipation.

We watched carefully as the next car made the steepest and longest drop of the ride, the passengers screaming with terror and delight. It plunged into the water for the big splash, which slowed it down so that it could drift up to the dock.

The man kept the chain on until all the people were out of the log car and off the platform. But as soon as he unhooked the chain, Jessica ran like crazy and made it to the front seats in a second. It took me a little longer to join her.

She shoved over and I stepped in. The car tipped forward, and the ride attendant rushed over to us, waving his arms.

"Sir! Sir! Would you please sit in the rear seats? For balance." He didn't come right out and say that I was too heavy to sit up front, and I was grateful for that.

"Okay," I said.

Jessica followed me to the rear seats. She got on first, then I stepped in. The car tipped again, but the man didn't seem upset by it. I pulled down the restraining bar to hold us in, and like the steering wheel of the Corolla, it dug into my belly, but I was too excited about the ride to get upset about it.

When the car was full and the attendant had checked that all the safety bars were in place, the log car pulled away from the platform and the ride started. If my weight slowed down the ride, I didn't notice, and I don't think anyone else did, either. We picked up speed, pulling out of the water and zipping over the rails, making sharp dips and turns that slid us from one side of the seat to the other. Jessica squealed with delight.

"You having fun?" I shouted over the noise and the air rushing into my ears.

"Yeah!" she said.

I knew we were getting close to the end—the steep drop and the big splash. As we crested the last incline before the drop, my stomach clenched and Jessica grabbed my arm. The car must have been at a sixty-degree angle, nose pointed down as we raced along the tracks. I yelled. Jessica yelled. It was terrific! I felt free and fast and light as a feather.

Then we hit the water for the big splash. Water shot out

from under the car and doused the people waiting in line. They shouted and yelled.

"Hey!" I heard one man shout. "Who let that guy on?"

I knew instantly that he was talking about me. The big splash had become the *really big splash* with me on board. I tried not to look at all the wet shirts and sopping hair as I got off the car and took the stairs off the platform.

I looked down at Jessica, waiting for her to say something, but she didn't say a word. We wandered out into the park, searching for our next ride.

"I want to go on that one," Jessica said. She pointed at what looked like a fairly tame ride. A car as big as a truck bed attached to a six-story steel pillar. The car gradually climbed up to the top, then dropped, stopping short before it hit the ground. It didn't drop all that fast, but Jessica really wanted to go on, so I agreed to do that one next. The line for this ride was short, so it wasn't long before we were on the car, getting into our seats.

"This is going to be good," Jessica said as she buckled her seat belt.

I had no idea why this ride appealed to her so much, but I was just happy that she was having fun. I took the seat next to her and reached for the seat belt, shifting from side to side until I found it. I pulled it around my belly and let it out all the way, but it was too short for me. I pulled and tugged, thinking it was caught somewhere, but it wasn't. I tried sucking in my gut, but I still needed another six inches or so to buckle it.

Oh, well, I thought, I don't need a seat belt for this ride. I dropped the ends and let them dangle under the seat.

"Can't fit, can't ride."

"Huh?"

"Can't fit, can't ride."

I looked up, and there stood a skinny man with a face like a prune and a scratchy sandpaper voice. He was a more grizzled version of Popeye.

"Can't fit, can't ride," he repeated. He was in charge of this ride, and he was checking to make sure everyone was buckled up.

I reeled in the ends of the seat belt to show him that it was too short for me, hoping he'd understand and cut me some slack.

But the rules were the rules, and he wasn't about to start making exceptions. "Can't fit, can't ride!" he said, raising his voice as if he thought the problem was with my hearing. He stood right in front of me, waiting for me to do something.

My face must have been ten shades of red. About a dozen other people were on the car, waiting for the ride to start, and they were all staring at me. I wanted to disappear.

"Can't fit, can't—"

"I heard you," I said.

I turned to my sister. She was frowning as if she'd done something wrong. "It's all right, Jess," I said. "Will you be all right by yourself?"

She nodded, still frowning. I could tell she felt bad for me.

"I'll wait for you by the ticket booth," I said.

"You sure?" she asked. "We don't have to do this ride."

"No, it's fine. I'll watch you."

I hauled myself up and got off the ride. I could feel everyone's eyes on me like a swarm of mosquitoes dive-bombing me and leaving welts on my skin. I didn't look back until I heard the ride starting. I couldn't bear to make eye contact with anyone who'd heard what that jerk had just said to me. I understood he was doing his job, but he didn't have to be so insensitive about it.

When the ride was over, Jessica found me at the ticket booth. She didn't say anything about what Popeye had said, but I could tell it was on her mind. I didn't bring it up, so we didn't talk about it. I decided not to try any more rides that day and risk further humiliation. I just watched Jessica.

We drove home late that afternoon, and she looked at me with sad cow eyes the whole way. I kept my eyes on the road. I didn't want to discuss it.

I suppose she told my parents about the incident, but they didn't bring it up, and I was grateful for that. But I don't think I'll ever forget Popeye's grouchy voice—"Can't fit, can't ride"—and how much that hurt me.

I vowed that day never to go to an amusement park again.

Popeye's voice was imprinted on my mind, and his hurtful words haunted me for years. I'd be lying if I said that wasn't part of the reason why I didn't tell anyone when I started the Subway diet. I didn't even tell JL at first. Fortunately, there were so many part-time student employees at my Subway shop that none of them picked up on what I was up to. Except for one girl.

I'm not sure if she was a student or not, but she was college-aged. She was petite and friendly with a smile that just never quit. She worked the evening shift and was always the first sandwich maker behind the counter, the one who took the bread order. I always came in at about the same time, and we kind of got to know one another. I knew from her name tag that her name was Laura.

Well, one night when I walked in, Laura already had a 12-inch whole-wheat roll cut open and ready for me.

"Veggie Delite," she said as I walked up to the counter. "No cheese. Spicy mustard. Everything except tomatoes, onions, and olives. Right?"

"You got it," I said.

As she made my sandwich, she suddenly looked at me, I mean, *really* looked at me. "Hey," she said, "have you lost weight? You look like you have."

I just shrugged. "I don't know."

But inside I was doing cartwheels. Someone had actually noticed. My Subway diet must've been working, I thought.

But I wasn't ready to hold a press conference. If I had lost some weight, it wasn't that much, not compared to what I had to lose.

I wasn't ready to say a word . . . yet.

Don't Tell Anyone

- Don't set yourself up for criticism that could discourage you from achieving your goal. Don't tell anyone about your program for change.
- Motivation must come from within.
- Keep your program for change a secret until you start to see some results—visible proof that others will recognize.

See the Big Picture

There is such a thing as having too much information. With some diets, people must spend a good deal of their time counting calories and fat grams and carbs and this thing and that thing. It's like trying to fill out your income tax return, except you have to do it every single day.

Every year publishers bring out dozens of new diet books. They also publish books *about* diet books, critiques and analyses of various diets, arguments for and against them. Magazines run hundreds of articles about dieting. The specialty magazines publish articles aimed at their target audiences—dieting for men, dieting for women, dieting for busy executives, for mommies, for kids, for teens, for hikers, for bodybuilders, for travelers. I've even seen books and articles about dieting for pets!

Some diets require a daily weigh-in. Dieters often become obsessed and start weighing themselves constantly, clutching their hearts with anticipation as they wait for their bathroom scales to give them the verdict. Have they been "good" or have they been "bad" that day? Have they lost or have they gained? If they discover that they're up a pound or two, they might go into a tailspin of depression. (And we know where that can lead.)

But this is all too much information. It does not help you reach your goal. In fact, it can get in your way and trip you up.

You do not have to be a crime-scene investigator when you're trying to make a big change in your life. You do not need to delve into the microscopic details of your situation. Achieving the big goal is not about compiling loads of tiny facts. As the saying goes, concentrate on the forest, not the individual trees.

Dieters should put their bathroom scales in the closet and forget about them while they're trying to lose weight. Instead, trust your clothes. They will tell you much more about the reality of your condition than the scale will. You already know how your jeans fit. I certainly did, and when I realized that I didn't have to struggle to button them any-more, I knew I was making progress.

I didn't buy any new clothes in the first few months of my Subway sandwich diet. I liked the feeling of roomy shirts and baggy pants. It was positive feedback that I was losing weight and a constant reminder to keep up the good work. Plus, loose-fitting clothing generally makes a person look slimmer. I'm not vain, but I must admit I checked myself out in the mirror from time to time, and even though I was still very overweight, I wasn't repulsed by what I saw. What I saw was me on the road to success.

When I finally did buy myself some new shirts, I discovered that I had gone from size 6XL (the biggest they make) to 4XL. Still pup-tent sizes, but I was absolutely thrilled. Just knowing that there were sizes bigger than what I wore filled me with glee.

When a person is trying to make a big change in his or her life, it's natural to become impatient. What you're doing is the biggest thing in your life. It occupies your thoughts all the time. So, of course, you want signs and signals that you're making progress. You want to know minute-by-minute that you're doing the right thing. Collecting information is the way most people make themselves feel that they're moving in the right direction.

But as I've said, having too much information can lead to discouragement, and discouragement can lead to quitting.

A smoker determined to kick the habit does not need to know the exact amount of nicotine she's not getting every day. She needs to know how she feels now that she's not smoking. After the initial withdrawal symptoms, does she feel better? Is she breathing easier? Can she walk up a flight of steps without gasping for breath?

A shopaholic does not need to check his bank account balance every day to see how much he is or isn't spending. Better to wait a couple of months and see if he has more money in the account now that he's been curbing his buying habits.

A parent having problems with his teenage son doesn't

need to read every teen psychology book on the market and second-guess the therapist he and his son are seeing. Better to follow the therapist's advice, give it time, and then look at the teenager's face. If things are getting better, it will register in his expression. And he'll probably see progress in his parent's face, too.

Remember, what matters is not how fast you progress, it's how *steadily* you progress. Fast starts lead to quick burnouts, but steady progress leads to permanent change.

Ignorance may or may not be bliss, but it *does* have its benefits. Knowing too much can be confusing, and if you're not getting the information you want to hear, it can stop you cold. When I started losing weight, I deliberately kept myself in the dark about some things.

One morning a couple of months after I started my Subway sandwich diet, I hung around the apartment, waiting for JL to leave. I knew his schedule, so I knew he'd be leaving for his biochemistry class soon. I sat in the living room, listening to him get ready for the day in his room. I was perusing that morning's sports section of the newspaper. The rest of the paper was spread out on the coffee table. The knife was under the business section.

I could hear JL rummaging around in his room. A few moments later JL charged out of his room with his backpack over his shoulder. JL had a decisive way about him, even when he walked. He always moved liked a man with a mission. I kept my eyes on the sports section even though I wasn't reading it. I forced myself not to look down at the sections of newspaper on the coffee table.

"Okay, I'm going to class," JL said as he reached for the doorknob. "See you later."

"Yeah, see you later."

He walked out and shut the door behind him.

I sat there and stayed very still, waiting to see if he'd come back. I knew what he was like. If he'd forgotten something—a book, a pen, his sunglasses, whatever—he'd figure it out right away and shoot back into the apartment to get it. I waited a full minute, then got up off the sofa and went to the front window. I spotted JL on the other side of the street, marching across the campus to his class.

It's safe, I thought. He won't be back. Even if he's forgotten something, he won't risk being late for biochem. That was his hardest class this semester.

I tossed the sports section onto the couch and reached down under the business section to get the knife. But suddenly I stopped myself and listened for footsteps. Just in case.

All I could hear was the sound of someone's car radio outside on the street. The pounding bass of heavy metal. Metallica, maybe.

I picked up the business section, and there it was, the black-handled steak knife, the sharpest one we had in the apartment. I stared at it, still listening intently for footsteps. It was quiet, except for that car radio in the distance.

I gathered up the newspaper sections and put them back together, then folded them in half. I sat down on the edge of the couch and positioned the newspaper in front of me on the coffee table. I stopped and listened again for footsteps, but there was nothing to hear. The car with the loud radio must have moved on, I thought. The apartment was eerily silent.

I took a deep breath, leaned back, and undid my belt buckle. I pulled the belt out of my pants and tossed it onto the coffee table. My heart started beating a little faster. I hoped I wouldn't mess this up.

I picked up the knife. Sunlight coming through the window glinted off the blade. I hoped it was sharp enough.

I leaned forward and put the end of my belt on top of the folded newspaper. Holding it steady, I considered what needed to be done. I took a deep breath and raised the knife, gripping it in my fist.

Do it, I told myself. Just do it.

I tightened my grip and brought the blade down, stabbing through the leather. I stared down at what I had done and decided that I'd hit a good spot. I leaned into the knife and twisted it, making the hole bigger.

I put down the knife, stood up, and started looping the belt through my jeans. Now my heart was beating harder. I felt around for the new hole with my index finger. When I found it, I started to buckle the belt. It took a little force to get it through, but when it finally went in, I was ecstatic. I was so happy I could have started singing.

I suspected that I had lost some weight, but I didn't dare get on a scale. I didn't want to know how much I weighed. My clothes were fitting more loosely, which indicated that I was losing weight, and that's all I needed to know. My pants had been falling down, and it had gotten to the point where I really had to do something about it, but I had been putting off cutting a new hole in my belt myself. The belt was pretty worn. If I messed up and ruined the belt, I'd have to go buy a new one, and I hated shopping for clothes, even something as simple as a belt. But I wouldn't have to do that now. Of course, that wasn't the reason for the incredible joy I was feeling. I had lost weight, and now I had proof. I had actually lost a few inches in my waist. The Subway diet was working!

But there was no way I was getting on a scale. Not yet. As far as I was concerned, I was still in the initial stages of this diet, the point when I usually crashed and burned. I wasn't willing to risk being disappointed again. That would be too devastating. I might never try dieting again if I blew it this time. Better to stay in the dark, I felt. At least for now.

I quietly continued with my Subway sandwich diet and didn't tell a soul about it. As the weeks went by, and the spring weather in Bloomington turned warmer, I could tell that something was happening to my body. My old clothes were fitting even more loosely. Shirts that had been tight across my chest were roomy now. Pants that had been snug in the thighs were starting to feel baggy. I could feel folds of extra material under my belt at the small of my back. And I was feeling better, too. Maybe not so much physically but certainly emotionally. I was making progress, more progress than I had with any other diet I had ever tried. And that felt good.

But I was *not* going to get on a scale. I did not want to know exactly how much I had lost.

What if I hadn't lost as much as I thought? What if it was all "water weight" and not fat? I'd heard a lot of overweight people talk about how easy it was to lose weight at the beginning of a diet because initially it's all "water weight." Losing fat is much harder, they all said. At 425 pounds, I probably had a lot of water in me, but in my mind losing water didn't really count. If I knew this was the case, I'd be disappointed, so I chose not to know and just keep doing what I was doing.

Having too much information and micromanaging my problem was not going to help me lose weight any faster. In fact, I suspected that it would do just the opposite. If I got on a scale every morning and didn't see pounds melting off at a regular pace, I would get discouraged and eventually stop dieting. I would start thinking about a Chinese buffet pig-out or a Meat Lover's pizza midnight snack or a Lumberjack Slam breakfast special, and I would surely succumb to temptation. Better to stay ignorant, I told myself. Just stay the course. Keep going. One meal at a time.

My clothes had been giving me a lot of positive feedback, and that was enough information, I felt. But by the end of the semester I stopped noticing my loose clothes the way I had at first. I wondered if I had hit that "water weight" wall. The water had disappeared, but the fat was still hanging on. I wondered if maybe I should break my rule and weigh myself, just to get a positive boost to keep me going.

But I resisted that urge. I knew that it was crucial that I not get discouraged. But I was torn. I didn't know what I should do.

Then one night I received a totally unexpected boost. I was slumped down on the couch with my bare feet up on the coffee table, watching television. The weather had turned unseasonably warm, and I was wearing shorts. I don't remember what show I was watching, but when the commercials came on, I happened to look at my ankles, and I suddenly noticed something. I actually had ankles again! The swelling had disappeared, the edema that my endocrinologist had warned me about, the sign of developing diabetes. It was gone!

I sat up and uncrossed my legs and took a good look at them. My legs used to look like logs, just as wide at the ankles as they were at the calves. But now they were tapered at the ankle the way legs were supposed to be.

I wanted to whoop and holler I was so happy. My health was improving. I might not have to worry about diabetes, I thought. That would be terrific. I was so elated, I missed the end of the show I'd been watching. I just stared at my ankles, admiring them.

But I was still cautious. The loss of swelling did not mean conclusively that I was out of woods as far as diabetes was concerned. Yes, my body was giving me positive messages, but I was still the big fat guy on campus. No one had mistaken me for Brad Pitt yet. But finally JL noticed.

It was around the time of midterms, and we were both studying hard. JL usually studied at his desk in his bedroom. I was too big for a small desk, so I usually spread out at the kitchen table. I was reading through my notes from my international-business class, highlighting the important stuff with a yellow marker, when JL walked in and went to the fridge for a glass of orange juice.

As he sipped his juice, he rolled his head around and rotated his shoulders. He was a complete exercise fanatic, and he was always stretching something. He just couldn't sit still.

Now one thing you have to understand about JL is that he's a real nose-to-the-grindstone kind of guy. He can be a lot of fun, but when he's studying, he's in the zone and that's all he does. When his nose is in a book, there could be a hundred naked girls in the apartment and he wouldn't notice. But he did notice something different about me.

He put his glass on the counter and went over to the doorway. He reached up and clung to the lip of the frame, bending his knees and doing a dead hang to stretch out his back. "Dude," he said, "have you lost a little weight?"

"Huh?" That took me by surprise.

"You look like you've lost some weight," he said.

I was embarrassed but also a little flattered. "Yeah, I guess so," I said. "Maybe a little."

"Maybe a little more than a little," he said. "What've you been doing? Another diet?"

I figured I had to 'fess up now. JL was persistent, and he'd bug me until he got an answer. His career goal was to become a doctor, so if I lied and said I wasn't dieting, I knew he'd hound me to get a checkup, thinking I was probably sick.

"You're gonna think this is crazy," I said, "but I figured out a diet for myself."

"Oh, yeah? So what're you doing?"

I told him all about my Subway sandwich diet.

His face collapsed as I started explaining. He looked at me as if I'd lost my mind.

I quickly gave him the facts and figures about the fat and calorie content of my two sandwiches, and suddenly he was a little less skeptical.

"Well, if it's working for you, man, that's terrific," he said. "And from what I can see, it's definitely working."

"Yeah, it seems to be."

"So how much have you lost?"

I shrugged. "Beats me."

"You haven't weighed yourself?"

"Nope."

"You're not curious?"

"Yeah, I am, but I'm not ready for that."

"How come?"

"Well, if I find out I've only lost a little, I'll be disappointed. I'd rather wait and get a big surprise."

JL looked a little puzzled. He was into science and medicine, and in his lab classes he was always looking for empirical evidence. "I guess I can understand how you feel," he said, but he sounded doubtful.

He let go of the door frame and stood up straight. "You know," he said, "I thought there was something going on with you."

"What do you mean?"

"I noticed it the other day, but I didn't say anything. It's in your eyes. You look—I don't know—happier."

That made me feel good. I was glad that he had noticed a change in me.

JL leaned against the wall and stretched his legs. "So do you want me to throw out my junk food? Get rid of the chips and stuff so it's not in the house?"

"No, that's okay," I said. "I'm learning how to resist temptation."

"You sure? I'll do it."

"There's junk food everywhere you look," I said. "You can't avoid it. I'm the one who has to learn how to drive by Mickey D's and Taco Bell and all those places. You know what I mean?"

"I hear you." JL went back to the counter for his juice. "You sure you don't want to get weighed, though?"

"I'm sure," I said.

JL went back to his room, and I went back to my notes. But there must have been a little smile on my face as I studied. Something good was happening to me. I just knew it.

I was more than a little nervous when the semester ended. I hadn't been home to my parents' house since the middle of March, and here it was, the beginning of June. I had lost weight, but I didn't know how much or how noticeable it was. I had a feeling my family was going to want me to get on a scale as soon as they saw me. My clothes were flapping around me, but I still wasn't sure I wanted to know how much I actually weighed. If I hadn't lost a significant amount—say, around 50 pounds—I knew I was going to be depressed.

My brother, Adam, was the only one home when I walked in the door in the middle of the afternoon, and even he was impressed in his own ultracool way.

He was sprawled on the couch in the living room, flipping through a magazine. "Hey," he said.

"Hey." I set down my duffel bag in the hallway.

He looked up from his magazine and gave me a funny look. "You look different," he said. "You lose weight?"

Even though we both went to the same college, IU is a big campus, and we didn't see that much of each other when we were there. He'd gotten a ride home with one of his buddies. I had driven home in the Corolla by myself.

"I might have lost a few pounds," I said and went back out to the car to carry more stuff in. I didn't want to get into a discussion about it with him. I knew that as soon as my mother got home, there'd be no avoiding the topic, and I didn't want to go over the same territory more times than I had to.

When I came back into the house, Adam was engrossed in his magazine and didn't pay any attention to me.

A little while later my mother came home. "Jared?" she called as she came in. She'd seen the car in the driveway so she knew I was there. "Where are you?"

"In the basement," I yelled from downstairs.

We met on the staircase, and her mouth fell open as soon as she saw me. I was afraid she'd faint and tumble down the stairs.

"Oh, my God! Jared, look at you!" she said. She was surprised and delighted to see the change in me. "Oh, Jared!" Tears welled in her eyes.

Later that evening when my father got home, she ambushed him in the front hallway.

"Norman, you have to take a look at Jared," she said excitedly. "He's in his room."

"Is something wrong?" he said.

"Just go look at him."

"Jared?" my father called out as he came up the stairs to my room where I was setting up my computer. When he got to the doorway, he stopped in his tracks. His eyes widened, and his expression gradually blossomed into a big smile. "Jared, you . . . you . . . you've lost weight."

I shrugged. "Yeah . . . maybe a little."

"More than just a little," he said. "How did you do it?"

I shrugged again. "I dunno. I just stopped eating bad stuff." I didn't want to tell my family about my sandwich diet. My instinct was to still keep the details of my program private. I was afraid they'd disapprove, and my father's disapproval carried the weight of his medical degree.

I managed to evade my father's questioning for a while, but when dinnertime came, I had a dilemma. Either I stuck to my Subway diet or I ate dinner with my family so they wouldn't know about it. It wasn't a choice, really. I knew that if I didn't get my Veggie Delite sandwich for dinner, I'd risk falling off the wagon. I'd gotten used to not having other food and hadn't tasted fatty flavors for three months. Eating my mother's home cooking could rekindle my desire for all the foods that had gotten me into trouble.

I stayed in my room and lay on my bed, reading a book. I hoped to avoid the dinner issue for as long as I could.

"Jared," my mother called up the staircase, "dinner will be ready in about half an hour."

"That's okay, Mom. I'm not hungry," I called back.

"I'm making meatloaf, corn, and mashed potatoes. Meatloaf is one of your favorites."

"I had a really big lunch," I said. "I'm not that hungry."

"You're not hungry?" she asked in disbelief. I hadn't been not hungry since I was seven.

She immediately yelled to my father, "Jared says he's not hungry. He says he doesn't want dinner."

Two seconds later my brother slid into my doorway like Tom Cruise in his sweat socks in *Risky Business*. "You're not hungry?" he said with a big goofy grin on his face. "You're not hungry? You're *always* hungry."

My mother shouldered past him and came into my room, followed by my father and sister. None of them could believe that I wasn't hungry. I laid the book on my chest and stared at them. Should I tell them or not? I wondered.

I sat up and put the book aside. "Well, to tell the truth, I have been on this diet. But it's kind of a different kind of diet."

"Oh?" my father said.

Yikes, I said to myself. This wasn't going to be easy to explain. But I did explain it, all of it. I even showed them a copy of the Subway pamphlet to support my argument.

Like JL, they all looked at me as if I were crazy. My parents' brows slanted back so far they were almost vertical. Jessica seemed confused. Adam, on the other hand, saw an opportunity.

"Obviously Jared has lost it," he said. "If he has to be committed to a loony bin, I think I should get the car full-time."

My father glared at him. "That's not funny, Adam."

He looked down at the floor. "Sorry," he said.

After a lot more discussion, I convinced them that I was not out of my mind, that I had put a lot of thought into what I was doing, and that it obviously seemed to be working.

"Well, then let's find out for sure," my father said. "Let's go down to my office right now and get you weighed."

This was *just* what I didn't want to do, but Dad quickly upped the ante.

"We can stop at the Subway out on the highway on the way back for your dinner sandwich," he said.

He was being supportive; they all were. Even Adam in his smart-ass way was pulling for me. So I couldn't refuse.

"Okay, but just the two of us," I said to my dad.

"Of course," he said. "You don't need an audience."

We left right away, my father promising my mother that we'd be back in time for dinner and I'd have my Veggie Delite with me so that I could eat with them. My father drove us in his car, and he tried to keep the conversation upbeat. I could tell that he was hopeful that I'd lost a substantial amount of weight. He knew how heavy I'd been when I'd seen the endocrinologist.

But frankly I was nervous. I worried that I'd find out I'd lost only a moderate amount and that he'd tell me it was all water weight. I worried about his scale, too. I knew that it only went up to 350 pounds. I imagined my father pushing the counterweights all the way to the right and the needle staying in the upper position, which meant I'd have to go back to the endocrinologist to use his scale. I still had lingering bad memories about that experience.

But there was no way out now, and I have to admit I was curious. I'd come up with this diet that everyone thought was crazy. It was time to find out if it really worked.

When we got to his office, my dad flipped on the lights, and we went directly to the examining room, where the scale was. I had butterflies in my stomach as I stepped on the scale, but it wasn't as bad as that last time at the endocrinologist's office, the day I found out I weighed 425 pounds. I knew I wasn't that heavy anymore. But how heavy was I?

My father started moving the larger counterweight, sliding it to the right. 200 . . . 250 . . .

Unlike the last time, I kept my eyes open.

300 . . .

350 . . .

My heart was ready to sink when something happened. The needle pointed *down*. There was too much weight on the bar to make it balance. Which meant I was . . . *under* 350!

My heart was pounding as my dad moved the large counterweight and brought it back to 300. The needle went into the up position. He started pushing the smaller weight across the bar.

5 . . . 10 . . . 15 . . . 20 . . . 25 . . . 30 . . . 35 . . .

The needle pointed down again.

He nudged the smaller weight back until the needle hovered in the middle position. I stared at it with laser beam eyes. 31. I weighed 331 pounds.

"Oh, my God," my father said. "You've lost 94 pounds in three months? I can't believe it."

"I can't either," I said blankly. I was so stunned I couldn't register an emotion yet.

My dad gripped my shoulders. "Jared, you're doing it! You're doing it!" He was so happy he had tears in his eyes.

It took a few moments for it to sink in, but as it did, my smile stretched wider and wider. He was right. I was finally doing it. My diet was working. I was losing weight!

See the Big Picture

- Too much information can be a bad thing when you're trying to make a big change in your life. Watching over every little detail of your situation can lead to discouragement, depression, and quitting.
- Trust your instincts. Gauge your progress by how you feel, not by the numbers.
- It's not how fast you progress; it's how steadily you progress. Fast starts lead to quick burnouts, but steady improvement leads to permanent change.

Throw Out Conventional Wisdom

Conventional wisdom tells us that a person cannot hope to lose weight without exercise. Changing your diet alone is not enough, we're told. You have to burn fat to lose fat.

Scientifically that's absolutely correct. Calories that enter the body as food have to be used or else they're stored as fat. However, your body is neither a furnace nor a science experiment. You have a brain. You have emotions. You have feelings, inklings, and intuition. I believe that sometimes these unquantifiable aspects of your personality can override what some would say is proven scientific fact.

I lost nearly 100 pounds without doing a lick of exercise. (Unless you consider carrying 425 pounds every waking moment exercise.) I think if I had tried to exercise I would have become discouraged and stopped dieting. I would never have lost the weight, and who knows how much additional weight I would have gained.

Exercise had always been frustrating and embarrassing for me. Having had to endure years of awful gym-class experiences, I automatically associated exercise with personal incompetence and humiliation. Exercising during the initial stages of my diet would have been a *negative* incentive for me to continue to diet.

If a program for change is nothing but drudgery, sacrifice, and discomfort, it's automatically doomed to fail. If you can't reach a comfort level with your program, then you won't follow it for very long. And if you do somehow manage to tough it out and reach your goal, you probably won't maintain it. Look at all the people who diet, lose a ton of weight, then gain it all back.

Supposedly knowledgeable people spout conventional wisdom and insist that an alcoholic can never come to grips with his or her problem without submitting to a twelve-step program, like Alcoholics Anonymous. But some people with drinking problems chafe at the religious aspects of AA, and as a result eventually stop attending meetings. AA has helped a great many people, but it's not for everyone.

There are all kinds of conventional-wisdom solutions for all kinds of problems. Psychotherapy for emotional problems. Mood-altering pharmaceuticals, like Prozac, for acute emotional problems. Nicotine gum and antidepressants like Wellbutrin for smokers. Ritalin and Adderall for attention deficit disorders. Relationship gurus appear on TV talk shows every day claiming to have *the* solution for marital problems, and some of their advice has become repeated so often it has become accepted, conventional wisdom.

But remember, what we generally consider conventional

wisdom started out as something put together for mass consumption. But you're not like everyone else and neither am I. None of us were made on an assembly line in a factory. So what works for one person will not necessarily work for you. *The program for change that **will** work for you must **come** from you. It must make **sense** to you. It must be tailored to fit your needs, goals, and individual situation.* Trying to make someone else's program fit into your life is like trying to wear someone else's clothes. Even if you wear the same size, they still might not feel right.

At my heaviest I couldn't even think about exercising. My back hurt all the time, and my joints constantly creaked and ached. Nearly everything I did was a physical ordeal. Just staying on my Subway diet was enough to contend with. I couldn't handle anything else at that point.

Of course, I wasn't inclined to exercise, either. Some of my most difficult experiences growing up involved exercise, sports, and gym class, and the bigger I got, the more I tried to avoid phys. ed. I dreaded taking off my shirt in public, so you can imagine how I felt about going into the boys' locker room to change into my gym clothes. By the time I was in high school, the experience became a twice-a-week recurring nightmare for me.

I wasn't thrilled about being seen in shorts and a T-shirt, either. It put too much of my body on display. My flesh jiggled, wiggled, and flopped when I moved, and in a tight-fitting T-shirt it was absolutely humiliating.

And what made it even worse were the girls looking at

me. My high-school gym classes were coed. It was bad enough being seen, but being seen by them was agony. Boys can be cruel, but in my experience girls can be savage. Some of the ones in my school were absolutely heartless with their dismissive looks, their laughing, and their snarky comments. They were like swarms of killer bees.

Every year we would have to take the President's Physical Fitness Test. The gym teachers would tell us it was coming up and make us do practice tests to get ready for the real test. Usually I could hang back in class and avoid most of the activities, but I couldn't get out of the test prep. It was mandatory. Even though it was painfully obvious that I couldn't do any of the items on the list—sit-ups, chin-ups, push-ups, sprinting, rope climbing—my gym teacher said I had to at least try. He said he had to get a "baseline score" on everyone to determine how much we improved when we took the test for real. It was required by the school board, he explained, and if you refused to take it, you would fail gym. I didn't want to have to go to summer school because I failed gym. Remedial gym—how lame would that be?

As the day of the pre-test came closer, I nearly developed an ulcer worrying about it. I'd get nauseous just imagining it. I'd be up all night, thinking of every conceivable nightmare scenario.

I'd get hurt.

I'd fall down and wouldn't be able to get up.

The gym teacher would yell and scream and force me to do things I just couldn't do.

The other boys would jeer and make nasty comments.

Worst of all, the killer-bee girls would laugh. I'd hear them in my mind. No matter what horribly embarrassing situation I came up with, they were always there, laughing at me.

I remember the first time I had to do that pre-test. It was even worse than I had imagined.

A royal-blue exercise mat had been dragged to a corner of the gym where my gym teacher would be conducting the tests. Each student would be tested alone. Everyone else in class had to play basketball until his or her name was called. One by one the gym teacher called out names, and students went over to the mat to be tested. The whole test took about five minutes, but for me it would be an eternity. I stood under one of the baskets, petrified that he'd call my name.

JL and a couple of other guys were shooting hoops, and I was retrieving the shots that fell through, tossing them back out to the perimeter. But except for JL, these guys didn't shoot very well, so I didn't have to do much retrieving. I wasn't paying much attention anyway. I was totally preoccupied with the test, stealing glances over at the blue mat, seeing who was being tested and how well that person was doing. Even the spazzes seemed to be doing better than I ever could.

I watched closely as one of the nerdiest kids in school did sit-ups. He was gawky and always seemed to be tripping over something. He hardly had any muscle on his bones at all, and his was *the* worst case of acne in the whole school. But he was doing it! One sit-up after another. I was totally astounded and envious as hell. I mean, I could barely bend over and tie my shoes sitting in a chair. There was no way I could lie down and do a sit-up, not even one.

The gym teacher held a stopwatch and told the nerdy kid when to stop. Like everyone else, he had one minute to do as many sit-ups as he could.

The nerd flipped onto his belly and started doing push-ups. Once again he surprised me. His form wasn't pretty, but he was doing it. I started counting as soon as he started. One . . . two . . . three . . . four . . .

His skinny arms trembled, but he kept going.

Five . . . six . . . seven . . .

His face was dark red, and his whole body shook, but he didn't quit. I couldn't take my eyes off him. I could never do that.

I kept counting, my eyes glued to him. Eight . . . nine . . . ten . . . eleven—

"Ooooow!"

The basketball hit me in the head. I watched it bouncing away from me, heading for the bleachers as I rubbed my scalp.

"Hey!" I shouted. "Who did that?"

JL stood at the foul line with his hands on his hips. "You're supposed to be paying attention, Jared," he said.

"That's no reason to hit me with the ball."

"I didn't do it on purpose," he said. "I made a basket. You're supposed to be returning shots."

"Well, I was," I said. "You could have given me a heads-up. I—"

"*Fogle, Jared!*"

I froze. My blood turned to ice water, and I suddenly felt like throwing up.

"*Next! Fogle, Jared.*" The gym teacher was calling for me. It was my turn to take the pre-test.

"Jared, go," JL said. "He's calling you."

All of a sudden the gym was quiet. No one was talking. No basketballs were bouncing. Everyone was either looking at me or deliberately *not* looking at me. I started walking slowly toward the blue mat. I wanted to run away, but of course if I could actually *run,* I wouldn't have been in this predicament.

The jocks smirked as I passed. The killer-bee girls buzzed to one another as they stared at me with predator eyes. The situation couldn't have been any worse.

"Come on, hurry up," the gym teacher shouted. "Let's go."

I walked as fast as my stiff legs let me.

"The rest of you get back to your games," he shouted to the class. "I want to see some hustle, or else I'll start marking off."

As I walked up to the blue mat, he smiled at me. "Come on, Jared. Let's give it a shot."

He held a clipboard, a pen, and his stopwatch. He had never been one of those mean gym teachers, and I actually kind of liked him. But I would have liked him better if he'd taught anything other than gym. Tall and well-built, he coached the basketball, tennis, and golf teams. I guessed he was probably in his early forties.

"Let's start with some chin-ups," he said, walking over toward the chin-up bar bolted to the wall.

He expected me to follow him, but I didn't move. Maybe there'd be a fire drill, I thought. That would be perfect.

He turned around and looked at me. "Come on, Jared. Let's go. I've got a lot of people to test today."

I nodded and headed toward the chin-up bar. It was about seven feet above the ground, and a folding chair had been set up nearby for the kids who couldn't jump that high. I was over six feet tall, but there was no way I could jump up even 12 inches and grab that bar.

But if I did somehow get up there, would the bar even hold me? Professional basketball players get cheers and standing ovations whenever they shatter the backboard going for a slam dunk. If I managed to tear the chin-up bar off the wall, I'd become a school legend. The kid who was so fat, he wrecked the chin-up bar. It wasn't a legacy I wanted to leave.

I stood under the bar and looked up at it. I reached up, stood on my toes, and was able to get the ends of my fingers around it. Over my shoulder I could hear the killer-bee girls snickering at me.

"I can't do this," I said.

"Try."

"I can't."

He gave me a sympathetic look. "I understand your situation, Jared, and if you don't do a single chin-up, that's okay. But if you don't try, I'm going to have to mark that as a refusal, and a refusal is a failure. I'll also have to report it to the principal, and you know what that means?"

I nodded. It meant detention and calling in my parents for a meeting about my behavior. I didn't want that.

"Okay, I'll try," I said. All I had to do was make an effort.

I bent my knees and tried to jump. I got my fingers all the way around the bar, but I couldn't hang on. My fingers slipped and I landed on my feet, pain shooting through my knees.

The killer bees tittered and buzzed behind me.

"I can't do it—"

"Use the chair," he said.

The chair looked sturdy, but I wondered if it was sturdy enough for me. I frowned at it, then looked at him, hoping for a reprieve.

"I'll spot you," he said.

Great, I thought. I would be known forever as the fat kid who fell on a gym teacher and killed him.

"Come on, Jared. I don't want to torture you. Let's just get it over with."

"Okay. I'll try." I put my foot up on the chair and tried to get my other foot up, but my knees said no.

He grabbed my arm for support, and with some difficulty I was able to get both feet on the chair.

"Okay, give it a shot," he said.

"Don't take the chair away," I said.

"I won't. Don't worry."

I gripped the bar, took a deep breath, and bent my aching knees until I was almost at a dead hang—almost, because the toes of my sneakers were still on the chair.

"Okay, try to pull yourself up," he said.

I tried, but it probably didn't look like it to him. Sweat trickled down my brow and into my eyes. My knuckles ached something terrible, and I could feel blisters forming on my palms. My shoulders popped with the strain as I shifted more of my weight from my feet to my hands.

"This is the best I can do," I said, wanting nothing in the whole world except for this to end.

"Great," he said. "You tried. That's the important thing."

But I was afraid to let go of the bar. I was afraid my knees would buckle.

He saw my dilemma and stood close, grabbing me around the thighs. "I've got you, Jared."

Was he crazy? I thought. I don't care how fit he is, he couldn't possibly hold me up.

The killer-bee girls laughed out loud. I glanced over my shoulder at them. They were clutching their stomachs and covering their mouths, getting a real charge out of making fun of me. I could feel my face flushing. I couldn't have been more embarrassed.

With my gym teacher's help, I was able to endure the pain and get down off the chair without falling. The mean girls were in stitches, and even the gym teacher's glare did little to quiet them down.

"Forget them," he said to me. "You're a brave guy, Jared. I have a lot of respect for you."

"Thanks," I said, huffing and puffing, bent over with my hands propped on my knees.

"Rest up a little," he said. "Then we'll try some situps. Okay?"

I closed my eyes. He had to be kidding.

But he wasn't, and I had to struggle through the rest of the test with the killer-bee girls and everyone else in the gym watching. It was so humiliating.

When it was all over, I had a perfect score. All zeros. Not one sit-up, not one push-up, not one chin-up. And the hundred-yard dash? I gave up after ten. And this was only the pre-test. I was going to have to go through this again for the real test.

The jock boys and the killer-bee girls thought my performance was hilarious, but I decided then and there that I would not give them an encore. The real test was scheduled for the next Thursday, so I faked a stomach virus that day and called in sick. On Friday the gym teacher gave me the test after school by myself without an audience. I will always be grateful to him for that.

I avoided physical activity in high school, but in college I just about banished it from my life, even after I started my serious dieting. When I'd learned that I'd lost 94 pounds on my self-styled Subway sandwich diet, I made an appointment with my endocrinologist to get a checkup, expecting him to tell me that I should start working out. I found out that my blood pressure as well as my cholesterol levels had gone down some. I wasn't out of the danger zone by any means, but I was showing some improvement.

The doctor asked me how I had lost the weight, and I told him exactly what I was doing. To my amazement, he approved.

"That's fine, Jared," he said. "It's working for you, so keep going."

He advised me to start taking a multivitamin every morning, which I did for a couple of weeks, but after a while I only took them when I thought of it, usually once or twice a week. The only thing I did religiously was get down to my local Subway sandwich shop twice a day for my turkey-sub lunch and my Veggie Delite dinner. I didn't exercise at all, didn't even try. People told me I should, but I knew that I couldn't do it. These self-proclaimed "experts" claimed that I would eventually hit a wall and stop losing weight unless I added regular exercise to my daily routine. But none of these people were morbidly obese, so they didn't understand. I didn't feel capable of doing anything strenuous or even "moderately active." Just walking was still a chore for me, and even the shortest distance put me out of breath and in need of a rest. I could feel that I was continuing to lose weight, and for the time being I was happy enough with that.

But when I got back to school in the fall of my third year, I had to face an issue that had been bothering me for over a year —my dependence on the campus bus. Walking was bad enough for me, but walking with a backpack full of textbooks and notebooks was nearly impossible. Most of my classes were no more than a five-minute walk away—five minutes for a normal person, that is. The bus route circled the whole campus, but the stop closest to my apartment went in the opposite direction, which meant I had to ride it for forty-five minutes before it got to my classes. I did this every day.

In the beginning I told myself that this was good studying time, but I was just kidding myself. It was nothing but a big waste of time. Worse than that, the bus had become my crutch. It was just something else that limited my already limited life. So when I got back to school that September, I set a goal for myself. I was going to start walking to class.

At this point in my life, I was more than just out of shape. I was in no shape at all. Even though I had dropped over a hundred pounds, I was pathetic when it came to physical exertion. With a backpack full of books, the longest I could walk was five minutes at a time, and I'd need a five-minute rest before I could start up again. Plus, everything hurt—my knees, my feet, my back, my shoulders, *everything*.

The first day I tried it, I thought I was going to die. My first class that day was criminal justice, which met on the eleventh floor of Ballantine Hall, about a twenty-minute walk from my apartment. It might as well have been a hundred miles away as far as I was concerned, but I was determined at least to try. It wasn't long after starting out that I was huffing and puffing, sweat spots showing on my shirt. I pushed myself to keep going, but soon I had to stop. I was out of breath, gasping for air, bending over with my hands on my thighs as other students breezed past me, heading for their classes.

A guy who lived in my apartment complex happened to walk by. We didn't really know one another, but I knew his face and, of course, everybody knew the fat guy from #1. He stopped and bent down to see my face. "Are you okay?" he asked.

"Yeah . . . fine," I said. I wasn't fine, but I was afraid

that if I complained even the least little bit, he'd call for an ambulance and tell the dispatcher I was having a heart attack.

"You sure?" he asked.

"Yeah. I'm okay. . . . Thanks for asking."

I appreciated his concern, but I wanted him to go away. I wanted to do this on my own, no fuss and no audience.

It took me forty minutes and four rest stops to make it to Ballantine Hall, which was only half a mile from my apartment. I stopped once more to get myself together before I went inside. My reflection in the glass doors was pathetic. I was so sweaty I looked like I'd just been doused with a garden hose. I was breathing hard and so tired I could've easily lain down on the grass and taken a nap. I frowned at my reflection. I knew I wasn't going to make it through an hour-long class without dozing off.

And that's when the campus bus pulled up to the curb. Students piled out and walked past me to get inside. I stared at the bus with mixed emotions. My bus pass was in my wallet. I could ride it back home after class instead of walking, I thought. But a wave of guilt swept over me. I didn't want to go back to taking the bus. But was I going to have to go through this every day? I wondered. That poor exhausted person looking back at me in the glass didn't look like he could take it.

I went inside and took the elevator up to my class and managed to stay awake through it. And to my surprise, I didn't feel half as bad as I thought I would. I decided not to take the bus. And I decided I would walk to my next class, and then walk back home in the afternoon . . . even if it killed me.

I forced myself to keep walking to class every day, and in a few weeks I didn't mind it so much. I still needed to rest but not as often, and as the fall weather turned cooler, I didn't sweat as much. I also found another personal spark that spurred me on to walk more—the campus bus. Every time I saw it go by, I felt more empowered. I didn't need it anymore. I'd thrown away that crutch. After about two months I was finally able to make it to Ballantine Hall without stopping once for a rest, and that day was a milestone for me. I celebrating by going home, taking out a pair of scissors, and cutting my bus pass in half.

Two days later I did that walk again without any stops, and this time I was only mildly winded when I got there. As I approached the front doors, I slowed down and stared up the length of the building. It was framed by a cloudless blue sky.

Eleven floors, I thought. And then I grinned.

That was going to be my next challenge, I decided. I was going to start taking the stairs up to my class. I would never dream of getting on a StairMaster, but this was something I wanted to do. And after all, I had to get up to the classroom.

And by the end of the semester, I *was* doing it—eleven floors, all the way up, three times a week.

Throw Out Conventional Wisdom

- Scientifically proven facts don't always take an individual's personality into account. Everyone is different, and each person reaches his or her goal for change differently.

- The program for change that will work for you must come from you. It must make sense to you. It must be tailored to fit your individual needs and goals.

Fill the Void

Separating the habit you want to kick from the rest of your life is probably the hardest part of any major life change. The bad habit doesn't exist in a box all by itself. It's a part of your life, entangled and ingrained in everything you do. Think of a big tangle of Christmas tree lights that were thrown in the storage box after the tree was taken down the year before. You can't just yank the strands apart. You have to sit down and painstakingly untangle each light in order to extricate the faulty strands from the ones that work. It takes time, patience, and dedication.

But separating the bad habit from all your good habits is just the beginning. Once you've eliminated destructive behaviors from your life, you'll find that you have a lot of time on your hands. What does an alcoholic do with himself when he doesn't go to bars anymore? What does a shopoholic do with all that extra time she used to spend at the mall? When couples stop their constant bickering, what do they do with their evenings?

There is no one-size-fits-all, all-purpose answer to this, and you have to figure out the solution that's going to work for you. In all practicality most of us won't take up radically new hobbies and lifestyles to fill the void. Few of us can afford the financial commitment involved with taking up parachuting, for example, or NASCAR racing or even nightly ballroom dancing lessons.

A more practical solution is to keep doing whatever you were doing before and learn to enjoy it *without* the addictive behavior that you've come to associate with it. In other words, untangle the string of damaged Christmas lights and get rid of it, so you can move on and decorate your tree.

Watch television *without* eating.

Go shopping *without* overspending. Maybe even leave your credit cards at home.

Go out to dinner *without* ordering an alcoholic drink.

Go to a rock concert *without* smoking a joint before the show.

Have dinner with your spouse *without* the nightly argument.

I know this isn't easy. But if you expect to conquer your problem and live a normal life afterward, it has to be done. Otherwise you'll be walking on eggshells wherever you go, waiting for the moment of weakness when the conditions conspire against you and you succumb to your addiction. The party, the concert, the restaurant, the night at home alone. You have to learn how to cope with these situations *without* your drug of choice, whether it's food, pot, or venting your anger.

It's not easy, but it can be done.

Obesity is not just a physical problem—it's a *lifestyle* problem. Overeating is not something I did only at meal-times. I did it all the time. My whole life revolved around food—getting it, eating it, and strategizing about how I could get more.

When I went from eating 10,000 calories a day to fewer than 2,000, I used to say half-jokingly that I had lost my best friend. But it wasn't really a joke. Food was my constant companion. We did everything together. If I watched TV, I usually had a big bag of chips and a liter of soda by my side. If I went out to a movie (back when I could still fit in a seat), an extra-large hot-buttered popcorn and a super-size soda were part of the deal. I snacked while I studied. If I had to go out on an errand in the car, I always stopped at a fast-food restaurant drive-through. My problem wasn't just the availability of fattening foods, it was how intertwined eating these foods had become with my daily routine.

A typical day for me at college when I lived in the dorm went something like this. I'd wake up around 8:00 A.M. and rush down to the cafeteria before it closed. I'd load up my plate with whatever hot breakfasts they were offering that day—eggs, pancakes, waffles, breakfast burritos, bacon, sausage, ham, hash browns, tater tots, whatever they had, and there was always a lot to choose from, so I took some of everything. I'd throw in a bagel or two, maybe a few slices of toast slathered with butter, cream cheese, or peanut butter. A couple of donuts if I was in the mood for something sweet. Coffee with cream and sugar, of course. And usually a few glasses of soda, and never diet soda. I didn't like the taste of diet drinks.

I'd drink cans of soda through the morning, even during class, and indulge in vending-machine snacks whenever I felt the urge.

By noon I was back at the cafeteria for lunch, and again there were always plenty of choices. Burgers, hot dogs, sloppy joes, pizza, chili, tacos, fried chicken, French fries. And that was just the hot line. The cold line offered all kinds of cold cuts and fixings for making sandwiches. I usually made my own sub on a long roll, stuffing it with mounds of roast beef and American cheese and ladling both sides of the bread with mayonnaise. The salad bar always had creamy potato salad, macaroni salad, and cole slaw as well as chopped lettuce, tomatoes, peppers, cucumbers, red onions, and various other veggies. I'd often make myself basically healthy salads, then drown them in creamy blue cheese dressing. Desserts were always plentiful—cookies, cake, pie, brownies, ice-cream bars, you name it. It was all there for the taking, and boy, did I take!

If I had an afternoon class, I'd bring another can of soda with me. By the middle of the afternoon, I was always a little hungry, so I'd stop at one of the snack bars on campus and order a burger, fries, and a soda or a milk shake just to tide me over until dinner.

Back at the dorm, I'd unwind in front of the television with a big bag of greasy, salty chips and some more soda.

Dinner in the cafeteria was a repeat of lunch except that the hot entrées were better—roast beef, spaghetti and meatballs, pork chops, ham steaks, mashed potatoes, and mixed vegetables that I'd dress up with lots of butter and salt. Some more salad with globs of creamy dressing, and maybe a rich dessert.

In the evenings while I studied, I always had an open can of soda near at hand. When I was finished studying, I'd get on the computer and play video games, which usually called for more snacking between games, a habit I had gotten into at home when I was younger.

By eleven o'clock I usually started thinking about my midnight snack. Pizza Hut delivered to the dorm, and as you know, I would regularly order an extra-large Meat Lover's with extra meat and extra cheese.

When I moved out of the dorm and took an apartment with JL, my eating habits didn't change very much. Cooking for ourselves didn't appeal to either of us, so we usually ate out, and for me it was almost always high-calorie, high-fat fast food.

As you can see, eating took up a great deal of my time. So when I started my Subway sandwich diet, I had a lot of hours to fill. The logical solution to that problem would be to do something else, like get a hobby. Well, that was easier said than done. Every recreational activity I enjoyed had some kind of association with food.

Whenever I watched TV or played video games, I snacked.

When I read a book or studied, I munched.

If I went to a football game, forget about it. There were

all kinds of concessions selling all kinds of foods. *Way* too many temptations.

If I went to the mall to go shopping, inevitably I would pass the food court, and just as inevitably I would find something irresistible that I just had to have.

If I went out for a drive in the car, I would eventually pass a fast-food restaurant that I just couldn't resist.

Okay, you might say, why didn't you do something different, Jared? Why didn't you try something new?

There weren't many sports I could participate in at my size. (Indiana University didn't have a sumo wrestling team.) And sedentary games like chess or Monopoly were too similar to video games to avoid the lure of snacking.

Dating was out of the question. I wasn't ready for that. And besides, everything a couple does on a typical date involves food—dinner out, a movie, a party. Food, food, and more food.

Speaking of parties, I'd never been much of a party guy. I didn't like the taste of beer, which was a good thing because beer is high in calories, and it seems to go all too well with pizza, chips, nuts, and sandwiches. If I drank beer, I'd probably just end up eating more.

I never smoked, thank God. Some people—particularly girls, it seems—take it up specifically to curb their appetites and lose weight. I was certainly no expert when it came to healthy living, but one thing I did know was that smoking in general is a very bad idea, and as a dieting aid, it's insane. Can you imagine how much harder it would have been for me to breathe if I had smoked cigarettes while carrying all that weight? I'm sure I would never have

had to worry about getting lung cancer because I'd probably have dropped dead of a heart attack before the cancer
had a chance to develop.

So what did I do to fill the void now that I wasn't eating
every ten minutes?

Well, nothing.

And everything.

Rather than overhauling my entire lifestyle, I kept it exactly the same. The only difference was that I did everything I did before but *without eating*.

When I started my Subway sandwich diet, I went cold
turkey (no pun intended). I felt that my situation was so
drastic, I couldn't afford to ease into a new pattern of
healthier eating. Going from three huge meals and constant
snacking to just three very modest meals was an enormous
change. Initially I was hungry all the time, so I needed distractions to take my mind off food. Unfortunately all my
favorite distractions matched perfectly with food.

I wracked my brain to come up with new activities that
would take my mind off eating, but I was stumped. I
couldn't handle any kind of physical activity, and I wasn't
willing to spend money on something I might not stick
with because I had a habit of starting things and quickly
getting bored with them. I lost interest in my courses easily,
and I can't tell you how many books I started reading and
never finished. I also needed something that would take up
a lot of my time. Ultimately I decided to concentrate on the
activities I was already comfortable with rather than seek
out new ones.

I started playing more video games and watching more TV to distract me from eating. I always made sure I had gallons of diet soda in the apartment. Whenever I got the urge to eat, I drank some diet soda, and that quelled the yearnings for a while. Over time I found that the cravings came less often, and becoming totally engrossed in *Super Mario* or *Grand Theft Auto* or the latest video release occupied my mind enough to keep me from snacking.

Surfing the Web could distract me for hours, but only if I stayed away from sites that dealt with food or dieting. I knew that there were numerous dieting chat rooms on the Web, and I avoided them all because talking about diets and cravings and eating strategies would not help me. If anything, this would set me back. I didn't consider that kind of commiseration supportive. I was afraid that listening to the woes of other people struggling with their weight issues would drag me down. And certainly I didn't need to hear pep talks from diet cheerleaders. That kind of ultra-positive happy talk would just turn me off. I knew that if I was going to succeed, the changes had to come from within myself.

I had spent five years at IU getting my bachelor's degree, and the fall and winter of my fourth year were the long haul of my dieting. I had made it through the summer at home and stuck to my Subway sandwich diet. When I got back to school, I was determined to keep going. Day after day I ate the same thing—coffee for breakfast, a 6-inch turkey sub for lunch, a 12-inch Veggie Delite for dinner, and a bag of baked chips or pretzels and a diet soda with each sandwich. Yes, it got boring sometimes, and yes, I was tempted to eat something else on occasion, but I stayed focused. I could feel that I was losing weight, and my diminishing body gave me the positive feedback I needed to stay the course. (The only time I varied my diet was on days, like Christmas, when Subway shops were closed, and even then I made sure I ate healthy, modest meals.) I also steadfastly refused to get weighed, except when I was at home and my parents insisted. By Christmas of that year, I was down to about 220 pounds. I was amazed and delighted, but I wasn't ready to rest. I was getting close to my dream—stepping on the scale and seeing it register below 200.

As the spring semester began, I fought the urge to get on a scale to see if I had reached my dream weight. I was afraid to find out, afraid that I'd be disappointed if I hadn't reached my goal. Maybe I had stalled, I thought. Maybe 220 was as far as I could go. Better not to know, I told myself. At least not yet. I kept eating my sandwiches and varied my diet only on very special occasions, and even then I was very careful and sparing about what I ate. I was happy enough with my new body and the feeling of energy and vitality I had acquired. I was walking everywhere now and had even started playing tennis again. And I was dating.

Losing nearly half my body weight didn't turn me into a campus Don Juan. Losing weight didn't change my personality either, but it did make me more confident in social settings. Ironically the first girl I asked out was a part-time assistant manager at the Subway shop in my building.

I took her out to dinner—no, not at a Subway—and had a few drinks with some of her friends. It was a nice enough evening out, but I think we both knew that we weren't meant for one another, so it ended after one date. But the best part about our date was that I had done it. I was definitely not the fat freak on campus anymore. I felt normal and perfectly capable of having an active social life. I was ready to start living.

One of the side effects of losing hundreds of pounds is that you don't look like the person you once were. Most of the people who knew me on campus knew me as the big fat guy. My hulking silhouette was enough for them to recognize me. But the enrollment at Indiana University is huge, and after I'd moved out of the dorms, I lost touch with a lot of the people I had known during my freshman and sophomore years, particularly my old dorm-mates. In a sense, losing weight had given me the cloak of anonymity.

One of the sweetest moments I experienced happened at an Italian restaurant in Bloomington. I'd gone out with a few friends. They all ordered big plates of pasta while I had a big salad. We were having a good time, telling jokes and trading stories, when someone from my past happened to come into the restaurant—Harry, a guy who had taunted me viciously when we had both lived in the dorm. I hadn't seen him in almost two years, and believe me, I hadn't missed him.

Harry had gained a little weight since I'd last seen him. He seemed chunkier and somehow squarer—square body, square head, square hands, even square shoes. He spotted us and immediately started walking toward our table. He knew most of the guys at the table from the dorm. I wasn't happy to see him, and I instantly braced myself. Back when we were living on the same floor, he always spewed out some kind of nasty remark when we met.

But I hadn't counted on one thing—he didn't recognize me. At first I thought he was snubbing me, but then he stopped and stared at me, squinting his beady little eyes. "Jared?" he said tentatively. "Is that you?"

"Yup. It's me."

His square jaw dropped open like the back of a dump truck. "What . . . what happened to you?" he said. "I didn't even know it was you."

I just smiled, feasting on the look of envy and disbelief on his face.

"How . . . how'd you do it?"

I shrugged. "I just went on a diet," I said and left it at that. As far as I was concerned, I was still on my diet, and the "tell no one" rule was still in effect.

None of the guys particularly liked Harry, so he soon went off to his table. But as we were leaving, I made a point of passing him as he slurped up spaghetti.

"Nice seeing you, Harry," I said as I headed for the front door. "Take it easy."

He looked up and stopped chewing, a strand of spaghetti dangling from the corner of his mouth. I waited for an insult to come out of him, but he was speechless.

As I walked away, I turned around and took one last look at Harry's face—the confusion, the jealousy. I wanted to savor the memory of it for a long time.

Another old acquaintance I ran into that semester was

Ryan Coleman. I also knew him from my time in the dorms. I was walking in front of the student center when I spotted him walking toward me.

"Hey, Ryan. How's it going, man?" I said as I approached him.

He gave me a funny look. I could tell he didn't recognize me.

"Jared Fogle," I said. "We lived on the same floor in Read Hall freshman year."

"Jared?" he said in disbelief. His eyes bugged as he looked me up and down.

We shook hands, but he kept looking at my body. "I can't believe it's you," he kept saying. "How'd you do it? Did you get your stomach stapled?"

I shook my head. "No, nothing like that."

"Then how? I mean—look at you."

Reluctantly I told him. By this point, I had suspended the "tell no one" rule because it was so obvious that I had lost a ton of weight.

"Subway sandwiches?" Ryan said. "That's absolutely incredible. Dude, I have got to write a story about you for the paper." He explained that he was now an editor for the daily campus newspaper.

I wasn't sure I wanted all that attention, but I have to admit, part of me was flattered. People had been marveling at what I had done, and I was beginning to believe that it was pretty remarkable myself. But did I really want to announce it in the school paper?

"Come on, man," Ryan coaxed. "You have to say yes. This is a fantastic story. It has to be told."

I thought about it, and it occurred to me that this might be a good incentive for keeping the weight off. How embarrassing would it be for me if I gained the weight back after showing off the trim Jared to the whole school?

"Okay," I finally said. "You can do the article."

Ryan was overjoyed. We agreed to meet a few days later so that he could interview me. "Do you have any pictures of you before you lost the weight? You know, at your heaviest."

I nodded. "Yeah, sure."

"Great. I'd like to run 'before' and 'after' photos. I'll get one of our photographers to take a good 'after' picture of you."

"Okay." I imagined what side-by-side photos of me would look like in the paper. I was sure it would be embarrassing, but it would also be positive feedback and most of all a good incentive to stay on the diet.

We shook hands and agreed to touch base before we met for the interview. We parted, and he started on his way. Suddenly he turned around and called to me. "By the way, exactly how much did you lose? How many pounds?"

I looked at him and shrugged. I was genuinely stumped. "I don't know. I'm not sure."

"Well, find out," he said as he walked backward. "I'll need that for the article. Talk to you soon." He turned and went on his way.

A hundred butterflies fluttered in my stomach. I wasn't sure I was ready to get weighed.

That evening I left the apartment at my usual time. "I'm going down to the Subway for dinner," I called out to JL who was in his room studying.

"Okay," he called back. "See you later."

But I didn't go directly to the Subway shop. I'd do that later. I passed right by, crossing the street and heading for campus. The gym was about a fifteen-minute walk. Even though I hadn't spent a whole lot of time there since I'd started at IU, I knew they had a doctor's scale in the men's locker room. I hoped there wouldn't be too many people there at dinnertime.

The locker room was mostly deserted when I walked in. I could hear showers running and voices in the shower room. A janitor mopped the floor near the pool entrance. A big round clock on the wall said that it was twenty after six. The scale was right under the clock.

I headed toward it, looking down the aisles of lockers as I walked to make sure no one I knew was there. If a friend or acquaintance spotted me, I wasn't going to do it. And if nasty Harry happened to be there, forget it. I'd turn around and walk out. I was sure that by this time he had come up with some barbed comments that he was saving for the next time we met.

But I didn't see a soul, only the janitor, and he didn't give me a second look. I went directly to the scale. I wanted to do it fast before whoever was in the shower came out.

I slid the counterweights to zero, kicked off my sneakers, and stepped onto the scale. The pointer clunked to the up position. I started moving the big counterweight, pushing it all the way to 200, and something weird happened. The needle pointed down.

This can't be right, I thought. The scale must be broken.

I moved the weight to 250 and the needle still pointed down.

I moved it to 150, and the needle pointed up.

Couldn't be, I thought. I'm between 150 and 200? No way. My pulse picked up a few beats, but I didn't want to get my hopes up.

The janitor was mopping his way in my direction.

"Excuse me," I said to him. "Is this scale broken?"

He stopped mopping and looked up at me. "That's the one the wrestling team uses. I haven't heard any complaints."

"Oh . . . okay."

The wrestling team competes in strict weight categories. They couldn't afford to use a faulty scale. A wrestler would lose by default if he tried to enter a bout in the wrong weight classification.

I left the big weight on the 150-pound notch and started pushing the small weight. Could this be the day I broke 200? I couldn't help but be hopeful, but I was skeptical, too. I couldn't possibly be under 200, could I?

I slid the small weight almost to the end of the bar, imagining my dream of seeing myself at 199, but the needle clunked into the down position. My heart started to thump. A thrill zinged through my stomach. I was under 199!

I nudged the small weight to the left, figuring I couldn't be much below 200. I moved it to 198, 197, 196 . . .

The needle still didn't move.

I nudged it a little more aggressively. 195, 190, 185 . . .

It didn't budge.

Oh, my God! I thought. This can't be.

184, 183, 182 . . .

No way!

181, 180, 179 . . .

Clink! The needle moved up.

I moved it back a pound to 180.

The needle drifted down and rocked in the middle position. 180. 180? Couldn't be. Impossible.

I slid the counterweights back to zero and stepped off the scale. Then I got back on and weighed myself again. The needle balanced at 180 again. I couldn't believe it. I weighed 180 pounds!

I was stunned. I couldn't stop staring at the floating needle. I checked the counterweights. Maybe I was reading it wrong. But I wasn't. It said I weighed 180.

"So is it accurate?" the janitor called to me from the doorway.

"Ah . . . yeah," I said a little nervously. "I guess it is."

Fill the Void

- The problem you're trying to conquer is not an isolated part of your life. Recognize that it has become ingrained in your lifestyle.
- People spend a lot of time indulging in their bad habits. Once a bad habit has been eliminated, that

time has to be filled by something else, otherwise it
will most likely return.

- Once you've achieved your goal, instead of re-
vamping your entire life, learn to live the way you
always have but *without* the addictive behavior.

LESSON 11

Change Is for Life

Suppose you were a gifted basketball player and your dream was to play in the NBA. What would you do? You'd probably practice hard in high school so that you could get into a college with a nationally ranked team. You'd train hard, eat the right things, condition your body so that you could play like a scoring machine and scouts from the pro teams would take notice of you. With a little bit of luck, you might be drafted by a pro team, and you'd be playing with the big boys. You would have made it. You would have reached your goal.

And then what?

Would you stop training and practicing? Would you slack off because you'd hit your target? Would you feel it was time to kick back and take a break?

Absolutely not. You'd have to maintain the level of playing that got you to the pros, so that you could stay there. You'd have to keep training and conditioning your body. Right?

Suppose you wanted to start your own business. You would most likely work day and night putting it together. You would refine the product or service you were offering. You would work long and hard on your business plan. You would scope out markets. You would court financial backers. You would contact potential customers and visit their offices. You would promote your business until you were ready to drop.

Now suppose your business started to take off. Customers put in large orders. Cash started to flow in. Happily you were forced to increase your staff and expand your manufacturing plant to meet the demand. All your hard work was paying off. Business was booming. What would you do then?

Take a couple of days off and play golf? Go on an extended vacation? Let your employees run things while you chilled?

I don't think so. Only an idiot would do that.

If you wanted your business to continue to succeed, you would keep on working hard to improve the business and maintain your market position. You'd set new goals and strive to meet them. You would want to prosper and grow.

So why should it be any different when you're trying to make a major change in your life? *The goal is not the end; it's the beginning, the beginning of a healthy life.*

Unfortunately, most dieters think just the opposite. They reach their target weight, and they can't wait to get back to "normal" eating. What they fail to realize is that what they were eating before was "abnormal" eating. What they ate during their diet should now be their definition of normal eating.

Dieters also get hung up in notions of rewards and punishments. If you think of your diet as punishment, let me break the bad news to you—you're doomed to gain back all the weight you lost. You will want a reward so badly, you will eventually succumb to fried onion rings and bacon-double-cheese burgers and chocolate layer cake and all those rewards you'd been denying yourself during your diet.

Recovering drug addicts and alcoholics understand this concept much better than dieters. A little snort of cocaine on special occasions would be absolutely out of the question for a former drug abuser. A couple of beers during the Super Bowl for a recovering alcoholic? Never. *Change is for life. Once you've kicked your bad habit, you don't go back to it. Not for any reason.*

It's true that compulsive eating is a little different from other addictions. You don't need drugs or alcohol in order to survive, but you do need food. But you must differentiate between good food and bad food. You don't need bad food to survive. Just the opposite. And the sooner you make that distinction, the happier and more successful you will be.

Great athletes, successful businesspeople, just about anyone who struggles and succeeds does not give up once the goal has been reached. *The real prize is **maintaining** that level of success, not simply reaching it once.* If you want to stay trim or sober or addiction-free, you must look into the mirror and tell yourself that this is your life now. There's no going back to what you used to think of as "normal."

If it were up to me, I would modify the words we use when we talk about making a big life change. Dieters talk about reaching their "goal," a word that implies scoring, putting a ball through the hoop, carrying a pigskin into the end zone, kicking a soccer ball into the net. You've scored the winning goal. The crowd roars. Game over. You've won.

Wrong.

That kind of victory exists in sports movies, but that's not how it works when you're dieting. If you think that you've reached the summit of your personal Mount Everest once you've gotten to your target weight, think again. Don't stick your flag in the snow and think the struggle has ended unless you want to be sorely disappointed later on. The struggle is not a temporary situation. The struggle is your life. If you don't learn how to live comfortably with that reality, you will inevitably fall off the mountain and tumble back down to where you started. In fact, you might even fall farther than your starting point.

It's a well-known fact that most people who lose significant amounts of weight eventually gain it all back and in many cases gain even more. Why? Because these people were willing to change their lives only *until* they lost the weight. Once they reached their goal, they drifted back to their old eating habits and consequently went back to their old body sizes.

This happens because the changes these people made

were not *for life*. They probably felt that while they were dieting, they were being deprived of "real" food. They felt that they were suffering through the diet and hated every single regulated low-cal, low-fat meal they ate. Once they reached their goal, they felt it was time to celebrate and do the equivalent of a touchdown dance in the end zone. In other words they fell off the wagon and fell hard. Health-shake breakfasts and salad lunches were all forgotten— hello, pizza and ice cream. Happy days were here again, these people thought. They invited all their "old friends" back.

The mistake seems so obvious. It seems that only an idiot could go back to his or her old habits, but believe it or not, even smart people fall into this trap. It starts with making a few small exceptions.

"I've lost 100 pounds, for God's sake. I can cheat just this once."

"It's Grandma's birthday. A little cake just this once won't hurt."

"I haven't had corn chips in so long, and they used to be my favorite. I'll just eat a few."

"I know I shouldn't indulge in a big Thanksgiving dinner, but my mother-in-law went to the trouble to make it and she'll be hurt if I don't eat something."

The small exceptions lead to bigger exceptions, which lead to more frequent exceptions, which lead right back to bad habits. Before long you're rummaging through the back of your closet, looking for the "fat pants" you wore before you started dieting.

When I found out that I was down to 180 pounds, I literally jumped for joy. But I didn't run down to the Chinese buffet to celebrate and break the fast. You see, I never thought of Subway sandwiches as starvation rations. I liked what I was eating all along. I didn't feel that I had to go back to "real" food. To me, these sandwiches *were* real food.

Before I stepped on the scale at the gym, I'd been having second thoughts about being the subject of an article in the school paper, but my fears evaporated as soon as I saw that I had reached my goal and significantly surpassed it. I was now looking forward to meeting Ryan Coleman for my interview and revealing that I weighed only 180 pounds. I couldn't wait to tell him that I had lost a grand total of *245 pounds in eleven months.*

I figured I'd cut out the article and send a copy to my parents and another one to my grandpa. I knew they'd all get a kick out of it. I imagined the article would be a small piece buried somewhere in the middle of the paper, and most people wouldn't even notice it.

The paper ran the article about a month after I had met with Ryan in April 1999. I was surprised to see it on the front page. The title was "From Thick to Thin." You couldn't miss the before and after pictures of me—big fat 425-pound Jared next to the slender 180-pound Jared. I'd never given it much thought before I saw these photos side by side, but I almost looked like two completely different people. I stared at the photos for a long time, taking stock of the change in me. I never wanted to go back to the old me.

When JL got home from class, I showed him the article, and we joked about my fifteen minutes of fame. I tossed the paper on my desk with the other copies I'd taken for my family and hit the books, ready to forget about the whole thing.

But the rest of the campus wasn't ready to forget about it. The paper had hit the stands in the morning, and though I didn't know it yet, by that afternoon I was the talk of the school. I left my apartment that evening, intending to go down to the Subway to get my Veggie Delite for dinner as I always did, but when I got there, I was stunned. I couldn't get in. I'd never seen so many people in there at one time. The line ran out the door and around the corner. Students who wanted to lose weight were clamoring for the "Jared sandwiches." As I stood outside trying to figure out what was going on, kids recognized me and called out to me:

"Jared, did you really eat just sandwiches?"

"What's the best sandwich for losing weight?"

"Did you eat any other sandwiches, Jared?"

"Can I have dessert on your diet?"

All of a sudden I'd gone from anonymous, self-styled dieter to a dieting expert. I smiled and waved as I backed toward the parking lot behind the building. I had a feeling I'd better drive to another Subway in town if I intended to get dinner that night.

I figured it would all blow over by the next day, but it didn't. When I started out for class the next morning, people recognized me. Some stared. Some called out my name and waved. Some came up to me and asked questions about my diet. It took me twice as long as it usually did to get to class, and it didn't end when I got into the classroom.

My professor was holding a copy of the newspaper. "Mr. Fogle," he said as I took my seat. "Our campus celebrity."

He started to applaud, and the class joined in with him, about thirty people in all. They all seemed genuinely happy for my success. I felt myself blushing because I wasn't used to this kind of attention. I'd always thought of dieting as a personal thing, something I kept to myself, but now I had gone public and it was out of my control.

"Thank you," I said, patting the air for them to stop. "Thank you."

The class eventually settled down, but I noticed one person whose applause was halfhearted, and her smile was forced. It was my friend Brenda.

Brenda was few years older than me and a business minor. We had been in a couple of classes together, and we'd gotten to know each other on the campus bus. We were both overweight, and that was our bond. She wasn't nearly as big as I had been, but she was what I would call stout— short and round. She had a sunny personality and a ready smile, but we hadn't gotten a chance to talk much since I'd stopped taking the bus and started walking to class.

Brenda, even more than JL, had kept track of my progress. She'd complimented me and encouraged me along the way and had also warned me about "plateau-ing," reaching a point in the dieting process where I just wouldn't lose any more no matter what I did. She said she'd been dieting for years, and no matter what she did, she always managed to plateau, then eventually gain all the weight back.

As far as I knew, I had never plateaued at any time during my diet. I figured I'd lost about a pound a day from day one. The topic had come up a few times when we rode the bus together, and she had warned me that it would happen to me eventually. She seemed sure of it. I'd hit a wall, she'd said, and I wouldn't be able to lose any more.

After class that day Brenda stopped me in the hallway. "I read the article," she said. "I'm really happy for you, Jared."

I detected a bittersweet note in her voice. I suspected that she was a little embarrassed that she'd been wrong about my inevitable plateauing. She might have also been a little bit jealous. I couldn't blame her if she was. If our situations had been reversed, I think I would have been envious.

"I've been watching you over the months," she said. "I think what you've done is remarkable."

"Thanks, Brenda," I said. "I appreciate your saying that. It means a lot to me."

"You're my inspiration," she said, flashing her sunny smile. "You're my hero." She laughed, but I could hear the sadness behind it.

"Thanks," I said, but inside I was feeling bad for her.

"I gotta run," she said. "See you around." She waved and hurried off to the elevator.

I wanted to say something encouraging, something that would give her hope, but I was at a loss. I felt a little guilty having succeeded where she had failed so many times, but that was silly, I told myself. Maybe I really would be an inspiration to her. Maybe now she would lose weight and keep it off. I hoped so.

One day a few weeks later I happened to be walking through the cafeteria at the student center, and I spotted Brenda sitting by herself. She was eating lunch, but she didn't look happy. On her tray was a plain garden salad. I knew from having eaten with her in the past that she never put dressing on her salads. Unless she was off her diet. She loved creamy Russian dressing, and I'd seen her drown her salads in it on a couple of occasions. A small cellophane-wrapped package of saltines still had one cracker in it. Two discarded hard-boiled egg yolks and the broken shell pieces were on the side of the tray along with a bottle of water, which told me that she was back on her diet. She looked so sad it broke my heart.

Seeing her like that told me so much. Brenda was not ready to change. She was making herself miserable, subsisting on foods that left her dissatisfied and deprived. She would never be able to eat like that for the rest of her life. Few people can. If she lost weight, it would be temporary because she would go back to Russian dressing and all the other foods she loved. Those were "normal" foods to her; what she was eating now wasn't. She hadn't found something that would work uniquely for her the way I had found Subway sandwiches, and so she wasn't going to change her outlook on healthy living. I imagined her losing and gaining for the rest of her life unless a change came from within. Brenda would be the poster girl for yo-yo dieting.

Things were never the same between us after the article was published. We were still friendly when we saw one another in class, but we didn't talk anymore, not the way we used to talk on the bus. The next semester we didn't have any classes together, and we sort of lost touch. On several occasions I thought about giving her a call just to say hi, but I always stopped myself, thinking she really didn't want to hear from me. Not the fit and trim me.

The brouhaha over the article died down after about a week or so. The day manager at the Subway shop in my building told me that business had definitely picked up, but it was nothing like it had been the day the article appeared. That had been their biggest day ever.

"We've got some new regular customers that we didn't have before, and we're selling a lot more of the Veggie Delites," he told me. "I guess some people are following your diet."

"Well, I hope it works for them," I said.

My parents and grandpa told me they enjoyed the article, but after a few weeks nobody talked about it anymore, and I forgot about it—until I got a call one evening from a very excited Ryan Coleman.

"Dude," he said, "you're never gonna believe this."

"Try me," I said.

"*Men's Health* magazine picked up the article."

"What? I don't understand."

"*Men's Health* is buying the rights to the article. They're gonna reprint it. We're going national, man."

From his ecstatic raving, I surmised that this was a good

thing. But after I'd thought about it, I figured it wouldn't really affect me very much. Just about everyone I knew in the world had already seen the article in the school paper. It wasn't going to make much difference to me.

When the article came out in *Men's Health,* it was a very abbreviated version. The magazine's editors had cut it down considerably and used it as a sidebar to a feature article called "Crazy Diets That Work." They changed my name to "Jason," and instead of using my before-and-after pictures, they ran a photo of a buff model with six-pack abs. I thought it was kind of funny—so much for "going national"—but Ryan got a byline in a major magazine, and I was happy for him.

I figured that was the end of it. I was happy with my weight and the fact that my life was on track. I kept eating my Subway sandwiches and had no intention of ever stopping. Sure, I ate other things from time to time—I wasn't fanatical about it anymore—but I had found something that worked for me and I liked it, and since I didn't want to ever go back to my old weight, I decided to stick with it.

The issue of *Men's Health* with "Jason's story" came out in the summer of 1999, and since my identity was completely disguised, there was no accompanying hullabaloo like the one that came with the original article in the school paper. Just as well, I thought. The fall semester would be starting soon, and my goal was to buckle down and concentrate on my studies.

School started, and things were pretty normal. But then one afternoon in early October the phone rang in our apartment. I picked it up.

"Hello?" I said.

"Hi. Is this Jared Fogle?"

"That's me."

"My name is Dan Dallin. I got your number from Ryan Coleman." He explained that he worked for the advertising agency that handled the Subway account. "Is Ryan's article about you accurate? You really lost 245 pounds in eleven months eating just Subway sandwiches?"

"It's true," I said.

"Aha . . ." I could almost hear the gears turning in his head. "Please don't take this the wrong way," he said, "but can you put two words together?"

"What?"

"You seem like a pretty articulate guy. Do you think you could talk about your diet for thirty seconds? You know, impromptu, straight from the heart?"

"I guess. But what's this all about?"

"Well, Subway has been getting dozens of letters from their franchisees, asking about you. We were thinking maybe you'd like to do an ad for us."

"An ad?"

"Yeah, a TV commercial."

My pulse started to race. "What would I have to do?"

"Just be you. On camera."

"I guess I could do that."

"How would you feel about flying out to Los Angeles for a couple of days for the shoot? All expenses paid over and above your fee."

Fee? Expenses paid? L.A.? My brain was zooming around the room.

"Mr. Fogle?" Dan Dallin said. "Are you there?"

"I . . . I . . ."

My heart was pumping in double-time. A trip to California? All expenses paid? I was having a hard time putting two words together.

Change Is for Life

- Achieving your goal is not the end of the road; it's the beginning, the beginning of the rest of your new life.
- Your program for change is not a temporary situation. To maintain the change you've achieved, you must make the program a part of your daily life.
- True success is maintaining your goal, not just reaching it.

LESSON 12

Move On with Your Life

Like it or not, the world around you is always changing and evolving. When you change, the world around you changes, too. Sometimes for the better. Sometimes not. There are two ways you can deal with change: Fight it and try to maintain the status quo. Or embrace it and try to make it work for you.

Fighting change is almost always a vain pursuit. And it doesn't really make sense if you've just succeeded in making a big change in your personal life. Change is good. So why fight other kinds of changes? Your resistance to change could set you back in your personal transformation.

The obvious example is the former drug addict who has kicked his habit but stubbornly refuses to stop hanging out with his old drug buddies because he doesn't want to be disloyal to his friends. But even if he has no intention of ever taking drugs again, just being around people who get high in places where drugs are readily available could cause him to backslide. He might still love these people, but the scene isn't good for him. It doesn't fit in with the change he's made in himself. If his drug buddies reject him for going straight, then it's really all for the best. It will take him out of a tempting environment that could ultimately set him back.

People who make big changes in their lives often end up feeling that they've lost their old friends. Well, this might sound harsh, but the friends who treat you differently because you've improved yourself aren't friends worth having. These people didn't appreciate you for who you really are. They saw you only as a fellow druggie, a gambling pal, a mad shopper, an eating buddy. Your true friends are the ones who see you for yourself, and they'll still be there after you accomplish your change.

Life is a roller coaster. You can go with it and enjoy the ride. Take the speeding dips and falls and plunges and make them your delight. But if you try to fight it, you're in for a horrific experience. You expect the roller coaster to go one way, but when it goes in another, you're rattled and upset. You might want it to slow down, then when it speeds up, you're scared. You might want it to stop, then when it drops precipitously, you scream in terror. And if you try to jump out, it could be disastrous.

Adopt the philosophy that it's all good. Change always presents opportunities. If you lose a friend, you now have time in your life to meet someone new. If you feel that you're no longer welcome at your old hangouts, you can now explore new ones. Life can be an adventure but only if you're willing to be an adventurer. Embrace the external changes and challenges that your personal transformation brings and move on with your life.

I lost my friend Brenda when we didn't have being over-weight in common anymore. I was sad to lose her, and I think she must have felt the same way. But that friendship was impossible to maintain with so many emotions in play at the same time. Deep down, she was probably feeling jealous and bitter that I had succeeded where she had failed. I'm guessing she also felt a little guilty for feeling that way. Whenever I ran into her, I felt awkward. I didn't know how to relate to her anymore. I remembered how people used to fumble to keep a conversation going with me when I was huge, how they treated me like a person with a handicap instead of just another person. But with Brenda, even something as simple as going for a cup of cof-fee was fraught with issues. If she put whole milk in her coffee and I put skim in mine, I could see that she took that as an implied criticism of her eating habits. It seems silly, but very often little things become big things in these kinds of situations.

Most people don't know how to deal with their obese friends and relatives. It might seem ridiculously obvious to say this, but just love and respect the obese person for who he or she is. And keep in mind that *pity is not the same as love*. Showing pity, no matter how well intended, is offen-sive to an obese person. Your pity tells them that you think less of them because of their condition.

Lecturing or advising an obese person about dieting is

another huge mistake. It's not as if they don't know they're carrying hundreds of pounds of excess weight. These people know what they look like, and they know very well that they have a problem—you don't need to tell them. There's not an obese person in the world who wants to be that way, and they're not burying their heads in the sand about it. Either they're not ready to deal with it yet, or they just don't know how.

If you get in an obese person's face about their problem, hoping that you can spur them to do something about it, I guarantee that it will backfire. Lasting change must come from within. Hounding doesn't help. When the person decides it's time to do something, then he will act.

Brenda wasn't the only person who drifted away when I lost all the weight. There were other people I knew—I prefer to call them acquaintances rather than friends—who related to me simply as the "fat guy." In their minds I was like Fat Albert or the typical fat kid on a sitcom. I was just a character in the group and more often than not, the butt of the joke. They never recognized the person underneath the fat, so when I lost the weight, they didn't know how to relate to me. Of course, most of them didn't care to try. As the pounds melted away, so did my relationships with most of these people.

But please don't get the impression that your world will inevitably change for the worse when you make a big personal change. Just the opposite. Doors that you thought were closed before will open up for you. You might never have even realized these opportunities existed because your condition had limited your world so drastically. My weight literally kept me out of places I would have otherwise enjoyed—movie theaters, airplanes, certain classrooms. And some of the limitations had been self-imposed. I didn't want to be mocked or criticized for my weight, so I avoided places where I thought that would happen. I couldn't imagine walking into a nightclub at 425 pounds. Even if no one said a word to me, I knew they'd be watching me, and I knew what they'd be thinking.

At 180 pounds I was free to go anywhere I wanted. I was mentally and spiritually free. I could go to the mall and not be stared at. I could buy clothes in any store instead of just the big and tall men's shop. I could go to a café and not have people stare at me, wondering how many sugars the fat guy was going to put in his coffee and what fattening pastry he was going to devour. Fat people are always being prejudged, and now I was free from that kind of prejudice. I was moving on.

I didn't know what to expect when the ad agency flew me out to L.A. to make a test commercial for Subway. I was a little nervous about being filmed, but most of all I was just wowed by the whole experience. Here I was, twenty years old, on my own in Hollywood with the company paying for everything. They even rented an SUV for me while I was there.

There wasn't much time for sightseeing, though. As soon as I picked up the SUV at the airport, I had to drive over to Universal Studios for a wardrobe fitting, which I thought was pretty funny. Dan Dallin from the ad agency had told me that they just wanted me to be myself in the commercial, but my own clothes wouldn't do. I needed the wardrobe department to supply me with "regular guy" clothes, which looked pretty much like what I wore all the time.

The biggest thrill was driving through the gates at Universal. A pass had been left for me at the car-rental agency, and I just showed it to the burly guard at the gate when I arrived. He checked his list, smiled, and waved me in. How cool was that?

As I drove to the building where the wardrobe department was located, a tram full of tourists passed by. Everyone on board gawked at me, thinking I was someone famous. The kids on board waved, and I waved back. A visible ripple of excitement went through the group of tourists. They were probably thinking the exact same thing I was thinking: This is awesome!

The fitting didn't take long, so I had the rest of the afternoon to tool around and take in the scene. But it was early to bed that night because besides being jet-lagged, I had to be on the set the next morning at 5:30 A.M., which was still early for me, despite the time change.

Everything on the set was new to me, but everyone was nice, particularly the woman from the ad agency who stayed with me and kept me from tripping over wires and getting in the way. I never realized how much work goes into making a short thirty-second commercial. And I never imagined that it took that many people, either. There had to have been at least thirty crew members that I could see, and probably several more behind the scenes.

What I found very interesting was the catering line. These people didn't call for pizza delivery or brown bag it.

Food was provided for everybody, and it was a spread that could compete with my family's annual family reunion celebration—except that the sandwiches were made with sourdough baguettes and croissants instead of plain old white bread and kaiser rolls. Fresh fruit was plentiful, but there were also mounds of brownies and chocolate chip cookies that disappeared in no time. I couldn't help but marvel at the incredible amount of fat and calories loaded onto that table. I'd always thought of Southern Californians, particularly people in the film industry, as health and beauty fanatics who existed on avocados and bean sprouts in sparing quantities washed down with massive amounts of imported bottled water. Well, these were the people behind the camera, and I guess they weren't that particular about what they ate.

Fortunately for me, because we were shooting a Subway commercial, there was also a wide assortment of Subway sandwiches for the taking. I noticed that there was a separate table off to the side with even more Subway sandwiches. I wandered over to check it out and saw the most perfect sandwiches I'd ever seen. The meats and cheeses were all neatly folded and symmetrical, and the lettuce, tomatoes, onions, and peppers were arranged as artfully as flower bouquets. Even the bread was perfect—no bumps or bubbles in the crust, no imperfections at all. I spotted a wonderful-looking Veggie Delite and started to reach for it when a young woman in an apron suddenly rushed over.

"No, no, no!" she called out. "Those aren't for eating."

She introduced herself and told me she was the food stylist. Her job was to make the sandwiches look as perfect as possible for the shoot. We talked for a while, and I found out that as appetizing as these sandwiches looked, they were hardly edible because of the lacquers, varnishes, and other chemicals she used to make them look fresh for hours on end under hot lights. I pulled out my pocket camera and asked if I could take her picture with her works of art. She smiled and said sure.

It took hours to get things set up, so I just wandered around, taking pictures of the director, the assistant director, the cameramen, the soundman, the make-up artist, the hair stylist, the production assistants—everyone. When we were finally set to go, I put away my camera, and we got down to the grueling business of doing the same thing over and over again. I never imagined that filming a commercial would be this hard, but nothing is taken for granted on a shoot, and every detail has to be just right. We did numerous takes, and I didn't even have any lines. (I didn't have to put two words together after all.) I'm sure it would have taken three times as long if they had given me some dialogue. I gained a new respect for actors and filmmakers that day. The public thinks of the jobs in the entertainment industry as basically a lot of fun, but it's a lot of work, too.

The commercial was simple in concept. As I walk into a Subway shop, the narrator says, "This is Jared. He used to weigh 425 pounds." A picture of me at my heaviest flashes on the screen. The narrator then explains how I lost 245 pounds on a steady diet of two low-fat, low-calorie Subway sandwiches a day. As he talks, I order a sandwich to go. I then take my sandwich and walk out of the shop. In the next shot I'm carrying my sandwich home to "my house," which was actually just the front of a house in a simulated suburb on a studio backlot. That was it, but it took a full day to shoot, and I was told it would take several weeks to edit and get final approval from the ad agency and Subway.

The day after we wrapped, I flew back home to Indianapolis. I was exhausted—I never really got on California time while I was there—but I'd really enjoyed myself. As soon as I got home, I had my photos developed and showed all my friends and family. It was cool to talk about it, but as with the newspaper and magazine articles, the novelty soon wore off, and I got back to my regular routine. As the weeks went by and I didn't hear from the ad agency, I just assumed that the commercial had been rejected for some reason and that was the end of that.

But then one day out of the blue I got a call from Dan Dallin. "We've got the commercial where we like it," he said, "and the test market results have been very positive. We're going to air it a few times in the Chicago market in December, then take it national during the Vikings-Cowboys game in January."

He gave me the exact date of the football game, and I wrote it down, but it all seemed so unreal to me. I hadn't seen the finished product, and I couldn't imagine my face on a few million TV sets between quarters of an NFL game. I marked the date on my 2000 calendar and tried not to think about it, which was like trying to ignore the elephant in the room. I thought about it all the time.

On the day of the Vikings-Cowboys game, I invited JL— who had graduated that spring—and a few other friends over to watch. It turned out to be a good game, and that almost distracted me from the nervous anticipation of waiting to see myself. Almost.

By the third quarter I started to think they'd changed their minds about airing the commercial, and the guys started to razz me, joking that I had made up the whole story. They were making a ruckus, giving me a hard time when suddenly a cola commercial ended and there I was on the TV set.

"Look!" I said. "It's me!"

They all shut up and watched. That half minute was totally unreal. It was me on the screen, but in a way it felt as if it wasn't me. I stared at myself, being hypercritical of the way I came off. Do I really look like that? I wondered. Is that how I walk? Do I really make gestures like that? I wasn't sure if I liked the TV version of me.

As soon as the commercial ended, my friends whooped and hollered. They slapped me on the back and gave me high fives.

"You're a star, Jared," JL said.

"Well, I don't know about that," I said.

"So where are the free sandwiches?" my brother, Adam, asked.

I laughed. "Dream on."

We all had a good time, but I figured that was it. Maybe Subway would pay to air it a few more times, but I probably wouldn't see it again. My fifteen minutes were definitely over, I thought. It was time to get back to being just plain old Jared Fogle.

Yeah, right . . .

Move On with Your Life

- When you make a change in your personal life, be prepared for change in the rest of your life.
- Your natural inclination will be to resist these changes, but that can endanger your personal transformation and trigger backsliding into your old bad habits.
- Friends who treat you differently because you've improved yourself aren't friends worth having. True friends are the ones who see you for yourself.
- When dealing with a friend or a loved one with a big problem, keep in mind that pity is not the same as love. Your pity is just another form of disapproval.
- Life can be an adventure but only if you're willing to be an adventurer. Embrace change and move on with your life.

The Harder You Work, the Luckier You Get

Finding a penny heads up or a four-leaf clover is supposed to bring you good luck, but in truth the only luck that makes a difference in your life is the "luck" you create for yourself. If you want something that really matters, work hard and get it for yourself.

Feed the flame deep within yourself, the burning desire to reach your goal. Make it your obsession and your passion. Pursue it relentlessly. In real life, nobody ever gets an unexpected check in the mail that makes him an instant millionaire. Buckle down and do whatever you have to do to achieve your goal. Discomfort, embarrassment, and ridicule don't matter. Ignore these things and keep telling yourself that you're doing what has to be done.

A surgeon can't heal a diseased heart without shedding some blood. A baby can't come into this world without an excruciating, messy effort. A skyscraper can't be built until the construction crew blasts a hole for the foundation and hauls the materials to the site, brick by brick, truckload by truckload. To bring about a major change in your life, you need to shed some blood, sweat, and tears. After you've achieved your goal, people will say how "lucky" you are. You might smile and thank them for the compliment, but inside you will know that it wasn't luck. It was hard work.

There are no guarantees in life, but I think it's pretty safe to say that people who think of themselves as losers tend to lose, and people who think of themselves as winners tend to win. History is full of people who thought big and made great accomplishments or overcame incredible adversity because they maintained a positive mind.

World champion bicyclist Lance Armstrong had testicular cancer that had spread all throughout his body by the time it was diagnosed. His chance of survival was so slim his doctors didn't even tell him the statistics. Against all odds, he swore to himself that he was going to beat his illness. He endured extreme treatments that ravaged his body and threatened to cause lasting damage. But he never gave up hope, even in his darkest hours. Eventually he licked his disease, then went on to win the world's toughest bike race, the month-long Tour de France. And he won it *seven times in a row*.

A pessimist might say that people like Lance Armstrong are just lucky. Even when a person like that is struck down by misfortune, luck rushes in and saves the day. "It's not the kind of thing that ever happens to average folks, like you and me," the pessimist says. This negative attitude is prevalent in society, and many of us buy into it even if we don't think we're being negative.

How many times have you heard or even used expressions like:

"She's so talented. It's in her genes."

"He's got everything. The guy was born with a silver spoon in his mouth."

"She always ends up landing on her feet. She's a born natural."

Most of us accept this concept of luck even if we're not aware of it. I used to feel that way. People who weren't obese were lucky, I thought, because they didn't know what obese people had to go through. But by extension I was telling myself that if people without weight problems were lucky, then I must be cursed. And if I was cursed, what was the use of trying to lose weight or get good grades or succeed in a career or meet a wonderful companion? My fate was set. I was born to lose.

Fortunately I was able to pull myself out of that rut. Deep within me I had always kept that spark kindled, the belief that someday I could do it, that I could lose the weight and live a normal life. The hard part for me was turning that spark into an action plan, which I eventually did. At no point did I look to luck, fate, gurus, patron saints, voodoo, magic wands, fairy godmothers, or any other external force, real or imagined, to get me out of my rut. I had to do it myself, and I had to work hard at it.

I don't believe in luck; I believe in hard work. When you work hard at achieving your goal, that's when you get "luck," if you want to call it that. I prefer to call it "success."

Perhaps the greatest challenge you face when you're trying to make a huge change in your life is believing that you can do it. People who have lived with big problems for a long time have little experience with good fortune. They feel like losers because they've forgotten what it's like to win. They sink deeper and deeper into their hole of despair. They withdraw from the world and seek comfort in the only things they know—food, drugs, alcohol, shopping, gambling, whatever. I know because I was there.

The way out for me was hard work, usually without positive feedback, not knowing for sure if I was losing weight or not. The key was keeping a positive frame of mind and believing that I was on the right track. At 425 pounds, I couldn't wait for luck to hit me. I had to make my own luck. And I did.

After I had lost all the weight, I discovered that I had developed an inner mechanism for making more luck. I had an ingrained positive attitude and a lot of experience at working hard to get what I wanted, so things just seemed to fall into place for me. Good things led to other good things, and pretty soon I was on a roll.

After my Subway commercial was aired, I figured my fifteen minutes of fame were over. Life would settle down, and I could go about my business being a regular, no-longer-obese guy. The commercial was first aired on a Sunday. On the Monday after, I got a few congratulatory calls from friends who'd seen it, but by Tuesday things had quieted down. But on Wednesday afternoon my phone started ringing off the hook. People from the ad agency were calling. People from Subway's corporate headquarters were calling. The response to the commercial had been "phenomenal." Franchise owners had reported a sudden jump in sales, saying that customers were coming into the shops asking for the "Jared sandwiches." The franchise owners started clamoring to have the commercial shown more often.

Subway responded to the demand, and sandwich sales increased around the country. The franchise owners unanimously claimed that it was all because of me. No one could really explain it, but for some reason people responded to me. I guess I just looked like a real person and they believed the message. Whatever the winning formula was, Subway was eager to repeat it, so they signed me up to do a few more commercials. For the new commercials they got rid of the narrator and let me do my own talking, which worked even better. Sales went up again.

I started getting comfortable with the commercial shoots, and I didn't have to be led around the sets anymore to keep me from tripping over wires. The new commercials were released over a period of months, and each time a new one was broadcast, the response was good. People who had never eaten at Subway before were coming in to give it a try. Naturally, Subway was happy, the franchisees were happy, and of course I was happy, too.

Over the years I've made more than thirty commercials for Subway. They've been aired nationally and in a few foreign countries as well. From time to time Subway tries other kinds of television commercials, but I've been told that when my commercials air, sales increase.

You might say I'm just a lucky guy. Or you might say that I worked hard to lose the weight and that people recognize how genuine my story is. When overweight people or people who just want to maintain a healthy lifestyle see me, they take my advice and eat Subway's low-calorie, low-fat sandwiches. Many people have tried my diet, and it's worked for them, helping them lose large amounts of weight. You can see some of these folks on the Subway Web site.

It seemed as if in no time I became a celebrity without even trying. Oprah Winfrey, who has always been keenly interested in the issues of obesity and weight loss, invited me to appear on her show. America had followed her long struggle to lose weight and cheered her on when she finally succeeded, so it was appropriate that I was invited.

I'll never forget the grand entrance her staff cooked up for me. They borrowed a photograph of me at my peak weight and enlarged it to a life-sized paper print tacked to a wooden frame. At the start of the show, Oprah talked a little bit about me and said that I had weighed 425 pounds but had undergone a miraculous transformation. A stagehand gave me my cue, and I stepped through the photograph of "fat Jared" and showed the world the 180-pound Jared. The audience was stunned into silence for a split second. Then came the applause and cheers, led by Oprah herself.

Even though I'd been filmed for the commercials, I had no experience with a live audience, so I was a little nervous, not knowing what to expect. But Oprah was great, and she let me tell my story the way I always told it, honest and straight from the heart.

But the big surprise of the hour came when Oprah called my best friend, JL, out on stage. I was absolutely floored. They'd secretly flown JL in from St. Louis, where he was attending medical school. I was glad to have him with me. We reminisced about our time together in high school and college, and I explained how JL had stuck by me throughout. JL talked about all the diets I had tried and how frustrating it had been for him to see me working so hard and getting no results. We must have conveyed the strength of our friendship to the audience because the final applause during the closing credits was thunderous.

Later that week I got a call from an executive at Subway, telling me that the day we appeared on *Oprah* was the biggest single sales day for Subway ever.

My fame—I'm still a little embarrassed to call it that— grew from there. I was asked to appear at a live theater show hosted by Triumph the Insult Comic Dog. Triumph is a hand puppet, a cigar-chomping rottweiler brought to life by his creator, Robert Smigel. Triumph speaks with a Yiddish accent and often works "blue," as they say, but in the tradition of insult comedians like Don Rickles, he is ab-

solutely hilarious, hurling nonstop insults and rude comments. I've been the butt of some of his humor on occasion,
but he's so funny, I can't bring myself to be offended.

For this particular show, which featured comic actor
Will Ferrell imitating singer Robert Goulet and the band
the Fountains of Wayne, I was supposed to enter the theater from the lobby after being introduced by Triumph,
and in a parody of my commercials, I was to toss Subway
sandwiches from a tray into the audience. I was told that
the sandwiches would be wrapped extra tight and taped so
that they wouldn't fall apart. Well, somehow those instruc-
tions didn't make it to the person in charge of the sandwiches. As I walked down the aisle, I reared back and
threw the first one like a football, and it unraveled in mid-
flight all over the audience. Ooops. I thought maybe that
one was a fluke, so I tried it again, tossing the next one un-
derhanded. But this sandwich came undone, too. Lettuce,
tomatoes, onions, peppers, and turkey rained down on the
audience, who shouted in protest. Smigel/Triumph came
up with some clever ad-libs on the spot and made the
"sandwich malfunction" look like it was planned, but I left
the rest of the sandwiches on the tray. I was afraid the audience would riot if I kept going.

The Comedy Central animated cartoon show *South
Park* featured me as a character in one episode. In the
show's typically irreverent style, trouble starts when the
kids of South Park misunderstand when they hear someone say that "Jared has aides," as in helpers. They hear it
as "Jared has AIDS," the disease. The "scandal" spreads

like wildfire, and the town goes crazy. But in the end the cartoon Jared calms everyone down and straightens it all out.

Over the past few years, various television shows and movies have made reference to me.

Brad Pitt made a guest appearance on *Friends* in which he played an old friend of Jennifer Aniston's who had been terribly overweight, but when he reappears in her life, he's a super hunk. She asks him how he lost all the weight, and he says, "I did the Subway diet, just like Jared. In fact, I did it *before* Jared."

In the movie *Austin Powers in Goldmember,* Mike Myers reprises his role as the slovenly sumo-sized Scotsman Fat Bastard, except this time around, Fat Bastard has dropped a ton of weight. In one scene he's in a movie theater, eating a sandwich, when Austin Powers asks him how he slimmed down. In his thick Scottish burr, Fat Bastard says, "I did it just like Jared, on the Subway diet."

On *Saturday Night Live,* comedian Jimmy Fallon appeared in a skit in which he played a Jared-like character who eats at a place called the "Sub Shack," where people go to *gain* weight.

I appeared as myself in the popular documentary *Super Size Me,* talking to filmmaker Morgan Spurlock, who ate nothing but McDonald's fast food for an entire month just to see how it would affect his body. The film is a chronicle of his thirty days of terrible eating, and it's a powerful illustration of what a high-fat, high-calorie diet can do in a very short period of time.

As a result of all this exposure, I'm often recognized on

the street. People will shout out, "Hey, Jared! Over here, Jared!" Others will run up with cameras and scraps of paper, clamoring to be photographed with me and get my autograph. I appreciate the recognition, but I like it much better when people just introduce themselves and shake my hand.

Occasionally this kind of fame can have its downside. I was at a Dave Matthews concert at Tiger Stadium in Detroit in 2002, waiting for the show to begin. I'm a big fan of the band, and I was really psyched for the show, especially because we had great seats down in front of the stage. But someone recognized me, and the word spread quickly. It wasn't long before the whole crowd in my section was chanting, "Jared! Jared! Jared!" Thankfully it stopped before the band took the stage, but as a precaution I left before the end of the show to avoid being swarmed.

All this public recognition has been great, but none of it compares to the day I was allowed to carry the Olympic torch on its way cross-country to the 2002 Winter Olympic Games in Salt Lake City. Though I only carried it for a quarter of a mile through the Broad Ripple section of Indianapolis, it took several weeks of preparation. I was asked to wear an all-white outfit, including a white hat and white gloves. I was instructed in how to carry the torch and how to keep it from going out. When the day came, I was thrumming with anticipation. The man who handed off the torch to me was in a wheelchair, and as soon as I took it from him, I could feel the presence of all the people who had carried it so far coursing through my body. I did a slow, deliberate jog, holding the torch over my head. The people who lined the route weren't looking at Jared the Subway guy; they were looking at the torch and what it symbolized just as they should have been. When I handed it off to the next person in the relay, I was still glowing with a warm feeling from being a small part of something great.

Once when I was on vacation in Hawaii, I happened to be standing in a hotel breakfast-buffet line when I noticed a shy little girl in front of me, hiding behind her daddy's legs. She must have been about four years old, and she was absolutely adorable. We made eye contact, and I waved to her. She immediately hid behind her father, then looked up at me to make sure I was still paying attention. We did this for a couple of minutes when her father finally figured out what was going on. He turned around, and that's when I realized that the little girl's father was Jerry Seinfeld.

I was speechless, but he wasn't. He squinted and pointed his finger at me. "I know who you are," he said. "You're Jared. From the commercials."

I bashfully admitted that he was right.

We shook hands, and he said, "You are the biggest thing in American pop culture."

Well, I didn't know exactly what to say to that, but when a mega celebrity like Jerry Seinfeld recognizes you, I guess that's something.

These brushes with big names have been a lot of fun, but there are some serious issues that need addressing in this country, and I always try to use my fame to do something constructive. The level of public ignorance concerning the most basic matters of health and diet is astounding. The vast majority of people in America has no idea how harmful a regular diet of Whoppers and Big Macs and just about everything else that's served in fast-food restaurants can be. Grocery stores are just as culpable because many of the products they sell are loaded with unnecessary fat and calories. Even some products marked "lite" or "healthy" fall into that category. I want everyone to be aware of what they're putting into their bodies, and I want to help them overcome the adverse effects of misinformed consumption.

In 2003 I was asked to participate in a panel discussion on childhood obesity at Harvard University Medical School. The doctors and other health professionals who attended were experts in their fields and knew all the facts and figures about obesity in children, but I had the experience and I was able to put a face on the problem. I told them my story and explained the role that food played in my life as I was growing up, and I think they came away from the conference with a new understanding of the emotions and thought processes that create young overeaters.

In association with Subway, I started the Subway F.R.E.S.H. Steps Campaign in 2004. F.R.E.S.H. stands for Feel Responsible, Energized, Satisfied, and Happy, and the program encourages families to learn about healthy eating choices and incorporate them into their lives. Our goal is to stop the increase in childhood obesity and help people achieve healthier futures. Today, one out of three children in America is overweight or at risk of becoming overweight. This is not acceptable. As part of the F.R.E.S.H. Steps Campaign, I speak at schools all around the country, spreading the word about the dangers of unhealthy eating. Everyplace I go there are lots of overweight kids and far too many obese kids, and it breaks my heart to see them. My story scares them—I can see it in their faces. But they need to be scared, and their parents do, too. No one should wait until they tip the scale at 400-plus pounds the way I did before they do something about it.

Another project I'm involved in is the Jared Foundation, a nonprofit corporation that raises money for programs that fight the spread of childhood obesity, particularly in the inner cities. Sad to say, but the rate of obesity is even higher among blacks, Hispanics, and Native Americans.

Children are not my only concern. I also participate in the American Heart Association's Heart Walk program, which raises money to combat heart disease and stroke. Heart Walks have taken place in more than 750 cities across the nation. Besides raising money, these 5K walks promote physical activity and heart-healthy living for the whole family. More than a million people participate in these events every year, and I'm proud to say that I lead walks as often as I can.

I continue to work hard at maintaining my weight, and my success has allowed me to help others improve their health as well. I feel privileged to have been given the opportunity to help others succeed. If you've been battling with your weight or any other problem in your life, I hope this book has inspired you and shown you how to make your own "good luck."

Be well, be healthy, and be happy.

The Harder You Work, the Luckier You Get

- Luck is a myth. If you want something that's really important, work hard and get it for yourself.
- Pursue your goal with passion. Never give up.
- Positive thinking and hard work are the real keys to success.

Jared's 13 Lessons for Changing Your Life, in Review

1. **Open your eyes.** Admitting that you have a problem is the first crucial step toward making big changes in your life.
2. **Do something.** When you're stuck in a rut, try something, anything, to get yourself out of it. Be willing to risk failure.
3. **Reach for the stars.** Set your sights high. Ambitious goals cannot be ignored. Be the hero of your own life and go for the gold.
4. **Find your personal spark.** Take a good hard look at your worst fears, then turn them inside out and make them work for you. For example, hang on to your fear that if you get any bigger, you'll have to start buying clothes at the big and tall men's shop or Lane Bryant. Think about that every time you're tempted to eat fattening, unhealthy foods.

5. **One size doesn't fit all.** Analyze your problem and create a plan of action that you feel will work uniquely for *you*. Think outside the box.

6. **Change your mind to change your life.** Get rid of preconceived notions that keep you from reaching your goal—such as, "Diet soda tastes bad" and "Feeling hunger is physically dangerous"—so that you can do what has to be done.

7. **Don't tell anyone.** You're doing this for yourself, not the rest of the world, so don't tell anyone about it at least until you start to see results. In this way you can avoid being embarrassed and discouraged by failure.

8. **See the big picture.** Having too much information can lead to quitting. Don't micromanage your situation, weighing yourself every day and judging yourself by what the scale says. Remember, it's not how fast you progress toward your goal, it's how steadily you progress.

9. **Throw out conventional wisdom.** Forget what everyone says you should do. If it doesn't make sense to you, it won't work. Follow the path that works for *you*.

10. **Fill the void.** Find distractions that will keep you from falling back into your old patterns and bad habits. This might involve eliminating the associations these diversions might have with the habits you want to kick. Remember, there's no law that says a movie can't be enjoyed without a bucket of hot-buttered popcorn and a liter of Coke.

11. **Change is for life.** Achieving your goal is not the end—

it's the beginning of a new life. Don't start slacking off now.

12. **Move on with your life.** Embrace the change in you, even if it means accepting changes in your personal relationships. Don't look back. Life is an adventure—take it.

13. **The harder you work, the luckier you get.** Luck doesn't fall out of the sky. You have to work hard and make your own luck. Keep working at it, and you will continue to reap the rewards.

Frequently Asked Questions

Wherever I travel, people stop and ask me how I lost all that weight and what my life is like now. Here are some of the questions I'm asked most frequently.

Q: What was your waist size when you weighed 425 pounds?

A: 60 inches.

Q: Did you *really* lose 245 pounds eating just Subway sandwiches?

A: Yes. I ate a 6-inch turkey sub for lunch and a 12-inch Veggie Delite for dinner, and I had diet soda and a small bag of baked chips or pretzels with each meal. I never put cheese, mayo, or oil on my sandwiches, just mustard, and I never snacked between meals.

Q: Which bread was your favorite?

A: Back in those days Subway offered only two choices: white and wheat. Nutritionally they're almost identical so I switched off between the two. From the time I was a kid, I've always loved bread. A lot of diets forbid carbohydrates, but my Subway diet allowed me to have one of my favorite foods, which helped me stick to my weight-loss program.

Q: Can I do what you did? Will it work for me?

A: There's no reason why it shouldn't, but you absolutely must consult your doctor and a dietician before you start any kind of weight-loss program. What works for one person might not work as well for another.

Q: Do I have to go to a Subway shop? Can't I make the same kind of sandwiches at home?

A: Sure, if you don't mind doing all the work. Cutting all those vegetables for the Veggie Delite will take some time and effort.

Q: Did you ever get sick of Subway sandwiches?

A: No, not really. I craved some variety in my diet sometimes, but I was motivated to lose weight, so I stuck with my two sandwich selections.

Q: Did you ever get cravings to snack?

A: In the beginning when I started the diet, I wanted to snack, but I fought the urges and stayed hungry until it was mealtime.

Q: Did people treat you differently after you lost the weight?

A: Yes, because I was almost a new person after I shed 245 pounds. The fat Jared was withdrawn and didn't get out much. The trim Jared got out more and eventually gained some fame. I think you can guess which version of me I prefer.

Q: You must have had a lot of sagging skin when you lost all that weight. What did you do about it?

A: Nothing. Most of it went away on its own because I was still young and my skin was very elastic. I never considered surgery to take care of the problem.

Q: Subway has added some new sandwiches since you went on your diet. What's your current favorite?

A: Sweet Onion Chicken Teriyaki. A 6-inch sandwich has just 380 calories and 5 grams of fat.

Q: What exactly is your relationship with Subway? Are you an employee?

A: I'm not an employee of the company or even their official spokesperson. I'm considered a freelance contractor.

Q: People must ask for your autograph all the time. What was the weirdest thing you ever autographed?

A: A man once asked me to autograph his pristine, vintage Model T Ford. I was very reluctant to do it, but he insisted, so I signed the hood with a black marker.

Q: Whenever you make a personal appearance, you bring along a huge pair of jeans to show how big you were. Were those pants really yours?

A: Yes, they were, and I take them with me wherever I go. I have to wash them every couple of months because I make so many appearances with them. They eventually start to smell even though no one wears them anymore.